T0395052

Fighter Aircraft of World War II

Fighter Aircraft of World War II

Heavy Fighters • Ground-attack • Naval • Jet Aircraft

Edward Ward

amber
BOOKS

Amber Books Ltd
United House
North Road
London N7 9DP
United Kingdom
www.amberbooks.co.uk
Facebook: amberbooks
YouTube: amberbooksltd
Instagram: amberbooksltd
X(Twitter): @amberbooks

ISBN: 978-1-83886-609-9

Project Editor: Michael Spilling
Design: Andrew Easton
Picture Research: Terry Forshaw

Printed in China

ARTWORK CREDITS:
All artworks courtesy Amber Books Ltd, except the following:

Edward Jackson (Artbyedo): 39 (lower), 48–51, 92, 142
Godzilla Graphics: 67, 186–187, 218–219
Rolando Ugolini: 74–75, 106–107, 120
Teasel Studios: 21, 57 (lower), 58, 59 (top), 64–65, 86, 87 (lower), 89 (top), 102, 103 (top), 119 (top), 122–123, 189, 192–193, 205, 209

Contents

Introduction

Fighter aircraft of World War II were of greater importance and produced in greater numbers than at any time before or since. Yet this was also a period of transition: piston engines reached their zenith just as jets made their first tentative appearance, radar began to supplement the human eye and biplanes were finally consigned to history.

Fighter aircraft had appeared for the first time during World War I, primarily to prevent reconnaissance aircraft from performing their missions unmolested, but soon began to fight each other. This led to strategically irrelevant but popularly appealing notions such as the 'dogfight' and the 'air ace' gaining a foothold in the popular imagination, and these ideals would carry over into World War II, where the fighter pilot became likely the most glamorous profession within the ranks of military personnel.

Thousands of fighter aircraft were in service in November 1918, but plummeting defence budgets in nations exhausted by war saw only modest development in fighter design and comparatively few new types produced in the first decade or so of peace. This would change in the early 1930s as political developments in Europe and Asia began to make war seem ever more likely and the revolutionary development in fighter design between 1930 and 1940 was astonishingly rapid, possibly even faster than during the conflict itself, when the most radical design developments had to be tempered by wartime realities such as materials supply, ease of production and strategic requirements. In May 1931, for example, the Hawker Fury, the first biplane fighter with a top speed greater than 320km/h (200mph), was introduced, yet by August 1939 the Heinkel He 178, the first jet aircraft, had flown and the first jet fighter designs were already on the drawing boards.

Left: A Kawasaki Ki-45 'Nick' heavy fighter – one of the Japanese Army's most effective high-altitude interceptors against US bombers such as the Boeing B-29 Superfortress.

The motion of its props causes an 'aura' to form around this US Navy Grumman F6F Hellcat aboard USS *Yorktown*.

By the time the He 178 first flew, the world had also had time to digest the experience of the Spanish Civil War, a precursor to World War I that would prove immensely influential. In Spain, biplane fighters were repeatedly unable to catch monoplane bombers and prompted a general move towards faster monoplane fighter aircraft that sacrificed agility, to some degree, to speed, climb and firepower. The relative success of agile biplane fighters in Spain combating other biplane fighters, however, saw Italy and the Soviet Union continue to pursue this design philosophy long after other Western European powers abandoned it.

By 1940, however, the vast majority of fighter designs were monoplanes, including the latest carrier aircraft, a field where until recently the high strength and slow landing speed of the biplane had been viewed as almost essential; but high speed and climb proved more important even within the naval sphere. The delivery of high speed was partly driven by aerodynamics but also by power, and the rapid development of the fighter aircraft was mirrored by the intense drive by engine manufacturers to deliver ever more power. This process

is illustrated nowhere better than in the case of the Rolls-Royce Merlin which, when fitted to early Spitfires, delivered 770kW (1030hp) in 1940, yet through constant aggressive development the same basic engine was producing 1540kW (2070hp), double the horsepower, in early 1945.

By that time the main emphasis had switched to the seemingly limitless potential offered by the jet engine,

though this was still in its infancy when the war ended.

At the same time, another technology had quietly revolutionized aerial combat, particularly at night: radar. For the first time pilots could 'see' through darkness and cloud to greater distances than ever before and in complete darkness. Suddenly, bombers that had previously been virtually immune from interception at night were both detectable and interceptable, leading to huge losses in nocturnal raids. One of the most persistent developments, however, was in the actual use of fighter aircraft, which by 1945 were increasingly being employed as close support assets supporting ground forces. Today, some 80 years later, ground attack remains a fundamental role of virtually all modern fighter aircraft.

Allies

On the outbreak of war, Poland and France were caught just as they were modernizing their air forces, causing Poland to fight with a totally obsolete fighter force, while France surrendered just as some potentially outstanding designs appeared. The UK had a head start by comparison in the Spitfire, but the Soviet Union and United States had both neglected fighter design. The Soviet Union was slow to adopt modern monoplane designs and the US maintained an almost pathological belief in the effectiveness of the strategic bomber to the detriment of other combat aircraft. Both nations would overcome initial setbacks after 1941 to produce huge numbers of the world's finest fighter aircraft.

Opposite: The Hurricane had proved crucial to victory in the Battle of Britain but by August 1941, when this photograph of 601 Squadron Mk.IIBs was taken, it was being replaced in the air superiority role by its great rival, the Spitfire.

Commonwealth Boomerang

Concerned about the supply of fighters from the UK and US being threatened, Australia designed its own, utilizing many existing parts and assemblies.

Powered by the Pratt & Whitney R-1830 Twin Wasp that was being produced under licence in Sydney for local manufacture of the Beaufighter, the design incorporated as many parts as possible from the existing Wirraway, a general-purpose two-seater derived from the T-6 Texan/Harvard trainer. The prototype Boomerang flew for the first time on 29 May 1942, proving both manoeuvrable and easy to fly,

These are CA-13s, or Boomerang Mk IIs, a slightly improved variant seen here over New Guinea with No. 5 Squadron RAAF.

Commonwealth CA-12 Boomerang

Weight: 3742kg (8249lb)
Dimensions: Length 7.77m (25ft 6in), Wingspan 10.97m (36ft), Height 2.92m (9ft 7in)
Powerplant: One 890kW (1200hp) Pratt & Whitney R-1830 Twin Wasp 14-cylinder air-cooled radial piston engine
Maximum speed: 491km/h (305mph)

Range: 1500km (930 miles)
Ceiling: 8800m (29,000ft)
Crew: 1
Armament: Two 20mm (0.79in) Hispano or CAC cannon and four 7.7mm (0.303in) Browning machine guns fixed, firing forward in wings

Opposite:
'Phooey' served in North Borneo during 1945 with No. 4 Squadron RAAF in support of the Australian Army's Borneo campaign.

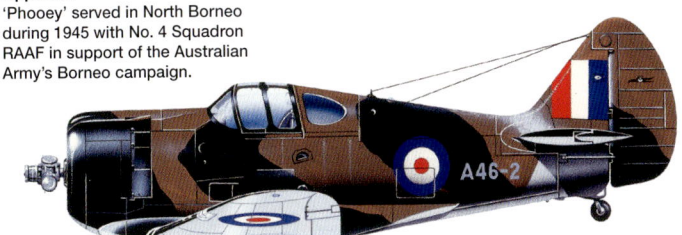

Above:
A46-2 was the second Boomerang to be built and wears standard roundels with the red central dot.

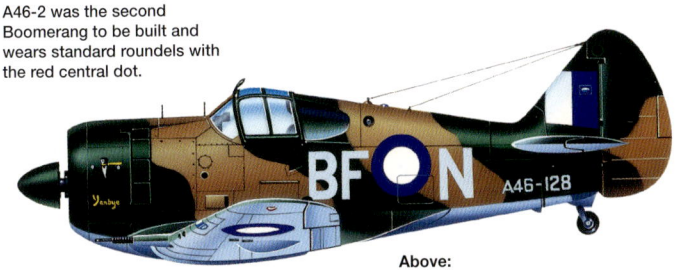

Above:
No. 5 Squadron flew the CA-12 from late 1943, primarily marking targets for other allied aircraft in New Guinea, New Britain, Bougainville and Borneo.

but was undeniably slow by international standards. Entering service in early 1943, there followed sporadic encounters with Japanese bombers over the next few months but the Boomerang simply wasn't fast enough to catch the enemy aircraft and no victories were attained.

However, once transferred to the close support role, the Boomerang was very successful. Agile, well armed and armoured, the Boomerang proved to be ideally suited to the campaign in the South West Pacific where small, close quarters actions were fought with indistinct front lines. Boomerangs were also used for artillery spotting, supply drops, anti-malarial spraying and target marking with small smoke bombs. The later production CA-19 tactical reconnaissance variant was equipped with vertical cameras and was heavily employed in action but the turbo-supercharged CA-14, which dellivered much improved speed and rate of climb, did not enter production or service.

13

Bloch MB.151 and 152

The Bloch MB.151 and 152 were produced concurrently and although they were not the most inspiring fighters in performance terms, they were very well armed and incredibly strong.

The MB.150 prototype did little to instil confidence as it actually failed to fly. After a redesign of the wing and undercarriage and the substitution of a more powerful engine, the aircraft managed to take off on 29 September 1937. The performance was sufficiently impressive to warrant further development and a pre-production batch of 25 was ordered. By 1938 France desperately required

German soldiers inspect an MB.152 that was shot down over France in 1940.

Bloch MB.152C.1

Weight: 2800kg (6173lb)
Dimensions: Length 9.1m (29ft 10in), Wingspan 10.54m (34ft 7in), Height 3.03m (9ft 11in)
Powerplant: One 805kW (1080hp) Gnome-Rhône 14N-25 14-cylinder air-cooled radial piston engine

Maximum speed: 509km/h (316mph)
Range: 600km (370 miles)
Ceiling: 10,000m (33,000ft)
Crew: 1
Armament: Two 20mm (0.79in) Hispano-Suiza HS.404 cannon and two or four 7.5mm (0.295in) MAC 1934 M39 machine guns in wings

Opposite:
A later production MB.152C-1 assigned to Groupe de Chasse (GC) I/8 in late April 1940.

Below:
Another GC II/8 aircraft, serving with the 3rd Escadrille. GC II/8 was charged with defending Dunkirk and achieved 21 confirmed victories before the armistice.

Above:
This MB.152C-1 flew with GC II/8 and wears the badge of the 4th Escadrille behind the cockpit.

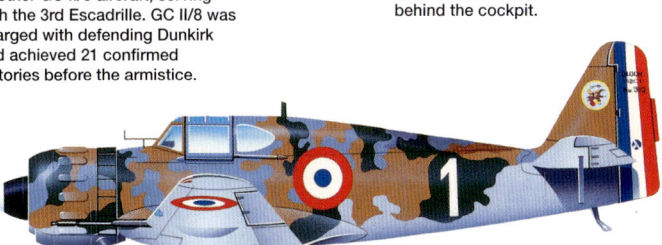

as many fighters as possible and the Bloch fighter was ordered in large numbers in MB.151 form with a slightly more powerful engine. These were joined on the production line by the further improved MB.152 but only a total of 85 aircraft had been delivered by September 1939 and none was combat ready. Eventually 593 were delivered, equipping eight fighter groups.

Combat record

In combat the Bloch's performance was adequate at best, being outmatched by the Bf 109E in almost every regard, but it did gain a reputation for remarkable toughness: one example that successfully landed after combat with 12 Bf 109s had 360 bullet holes. During the Battle for France, Bloch fighters claimed 188 victories for the loss of 86. The type was also exported in small numbers to Greece, the nine examples that were delivered seeing intense action during the invasion of Greece in 1940 and 41.

Dewoitine D.520

Generally considered the best of the French fighter types to make it into action, the D.520 continued to serve long after the armistice in both Axis and Allied air forces.

The D.520 saw combat in significant numbers before the June 1940 armistice but only just. The aircraft made its first flight in October 1938 and the programme was delayed after the prototype was damaged on landing after the test pilot forgot to lower the undercarriage. The first production aircraft appeared as late as November 1939 but Dewoitine had deliberately engineered the

The white fuselage arrow and roundel surround denote that this D.520 was photographed while in Vichy French service.

Dewoitine D.520C.1

Weight: 2677kg (5902lb)
Dimensions: Length 8.6m (28ft 3in), Wingspan 10.2m (33ft 6in), Height 2.57m (8ft 5in)
Powerplant: One 967kW (935hp) Hispano-Suiza 12Y-45 V-12 liquid cooled piston engine
Speed: 560km/h (350mph)
Range: 1250km (780 miles)

Ceiling: 10,000m (33,000ft)
Crew: 1
Armament: One 20mm (0.79in) Hispano-Suiza HS.404 cannon firing through propeller hub and four 7.5mm (0.295in) MAC 1934 machine guns in wings

All images:
From June 1941 Vichy France adopted red and yellow stripes for its aircraft but the treatment of the nose stripes of this D.520 is highly unusual. The aircraft was serving with GC II/7 at Gabes, Tunisia, in April 1942.

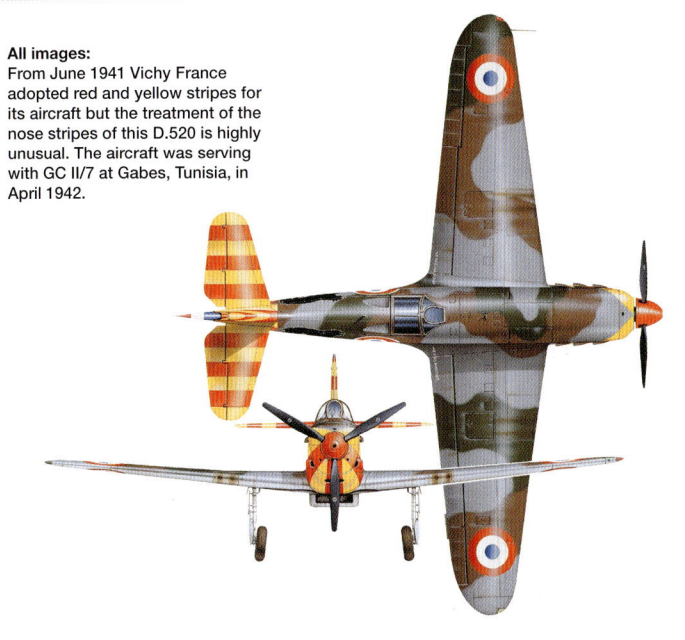

D.520 to be comparatively easy to build and by June 1940 300 aircraft a month were being constructed. Compared to the Bf 109E, expected to be its main opponent, the D.520 was 32km/h (20mph) slower but could outmanoeuvre the German aircraft and was well armed. However, during the Battle of France, most of the D.520's air combat was against Italian aircraft and the aircraft was superior to all *Regia Aeronautica* fighters then in service.

Vichy fighter

Following the capitulation D.520s became the standard Vichy fighter type, the German authorities having permitted production to restart, and saw action against the Allies in Syria and Tunisia. After D-Day, however, Free French D.520s went into action in Southern France against pockets of German resistance. The Germans also supplied around 100 captured D.520s to Bulgaria and 60 D.520s to Italy, and these were used by both nations to intercept American and British bombing raids, achieving several victories.

Morane-Saulnier MS.406

The most numerically important French fighter during the Battle for France, the MS.406 was pleasant to fly and manoeuvrable but struggled against the faster Bf 109.

The MS.406 represented a radical change for Morane-Saulnier as it was their first fighter design that was not a strut-braced parasol monoplane as well as their first design to feature an enclosed cockpit and retractable undercarriage. The aircraft did not feature stressed skin construction but utilized a bonded plywood and duralumin sheet called 'Plymax' fixed to a metal frame.

Forty-one examples of the re-engined Finnish Mörkö conversion were built. The roundel carried by these Mörkös dates the photograph to September 1944 or later.

Morane-Saulnier MS.406C1

Weight: 2540kg (5600lb)
Dimensions: Length 8.17m (26ft 10in), Wingspan 10.61m (34ft 10in), Height 3.25m (10ft 8in)
Powerplant: One 640kW (860hp) Hispano-Suiza 12Y-31 V-12 liquid-cooled piston engine
Maximum speed: 490km/h (304mph)

Range: 1100km (680 miles)
Ceiling: 9400m (30,800ft)
Crew: 1
Armament: One 20mm (0.79in) Hispano-Suiza HS.404 cannon firing through propeller hub and two 7.5mm (0.295in) MAC 1934 machine guns in wings

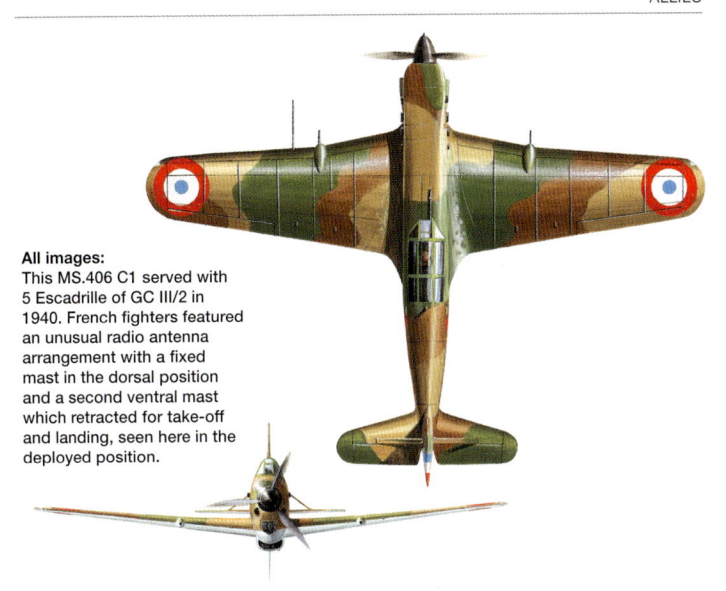

All images:
This MS.406 C1 served with 5 Escadrille of GC III/2 in 1940. French fighters featured an unusual radio antenna arrangement with a fixed mast in the dorsal position and a second ventral mast which retracted for take-off and landing, seen here in the deployed position.

The prototype, designated MS.405, flew in August 1935 and demonstrated a suitably impressive performance to be ordered into production with a modified wing, as the MS.406. Production, although initially slow, had increased to 11 aircraft a day by the outbreak of war when over 500 were in service and 1176 were constructed in total. In combat over France, the MS.406 was generally outclassed by the Bf 109E, which was 100km/h (60mph) faster though it could outmanoeuvre the German machine, and around 150 were lost in aerial combat, in exchange for 191 confirmed victories.

Export model

The MS.406 was also exported in small numbers, before the war, to Finland, which subsequently received further captured aircraft from Germany, where they saw long and effective service. To maintain their competitiveness, Finnish MS.406s were re-engined with captured Russian Klimov M-105 engines to produce the *Mörkö-Morane* ('*Bogeyman-Morane*'). Switzerland also operated MS.406s, building 84 examples under licence before developing the improved D.3800 series, used as a trainer until 1959.

Potez 630 and 631

> The multirole Potez was France's take on the vogue for the 'heavy fighter' that was prevalent in the 1930s but proved a largely ineffectual combat aircraft.

An exceptionally well designed machine, the twin engine Potez could be built more cheaply and in fewer man hours than the Morane-Saulnier 406 and could be used for a far wider variety of tasks than any single-engined, single-seat fighter. Formulated in response to a 1934 specification calling for a heavy fighter and close support aircraft, the Potez 630-01 prototype made its

Factory-fresh Potez fighters await delivery to operational units. The Potez twin was a fine handling aircraft but by 1939 it lacked sufficient performance to survive.

Potez 631

Weight: 3735kg (8235lb)
Dimensions: Length 11.07m (36ft 4in), Wingspan 16m (52ft 6in), Height 3.6m (11ft 10in)
Powerplant: Two 522kW (700 hp) Gnome-Rhône 14M 14-cylinder air-cooled radial engines
Maximum speed: 440km/h (273mph)

Ceiling: 10,000m (32,800ft)
Crew: 2 or 3
Armament: Two 20mm (0.79in) Hispano 404 cannon in ventral fuselage. One forward firing and one rearward firing 7.5mm (0.295in) MAC 1934 fixed in wing, one 7.5mm (0.295in) MAC 1934 flexibly mounted in rear cockpit

Opposite:
Romania bought 20 Potez 633s in 1939, including this one. However, in November 1942, German units occupied Vichy bases and seized their aircraft. Fifty-three further Potez twins were refurbished and delivered to Romania.

Above & below:
The 630 family achieved a number of prewar export sales to Romania, Greece, Hungary and Poland as well as Switzerland, which obtained two aircraft, a 632 bomber and this Potez 630 C3 fighter, based at Dübendorf airfield.

first flight on 25 April 1936 and was followed by the 633 bomber variant and the specialized 63.11 reconnaissance derivative, the latter becoming the most numerous version of the basic design.

Slow type

Unfortunately it never possessed engines with sufficient power, neither the unreliable Hispano-Suiza 14 of the Potez 630, nor the Gnome-Rhône 14M fitted to the Potez 631, and its performance was inadequate for the fighter role: several German bomber designs could outrun it and the Bf 109E was a full 130km/h (80mph) faster. Only four confirmed victories were attained by the Potez 631 in *Armee de l'air* service, for the loss of 10 of their own, but the two *Aeronavale* Potez units had more success over the North Sea, shooting down 12 enemy aircraft while losing eight. A particular problem for the Potez twin was its close resemblance in outline to the Bf 110 and at least three were lost to French 'friendly fire'.

Fokker D.XXI

Simple, rugged and dependable, the D.XXI was the most modern Dutch single-seater to operate during the Second World War, seeing most of its service with Finland

Designed to the requirements of the Royal Netherlands East Indies Army Air Force, the D.XXI was a modern low-wing cantilever monoplane with an enclosed cockpit but did not feature retractable undercarriage. The aircraft made its first flight on 27 March 1936 and 36 were ordered for the Netherlands Air Force. Seven D.XXIs were purchased by Finland, which also acquired a manufacturing

Prototype D.XXI, here in prewar Dutch markings that would be replaced by orange triangle 'neutrality markings' after September 1939.

Fokker D.XXI

Weight: 2050kg (4519lb)
Dimensions: Length 8.2m (26ft 11in), Wingspan 11m (36ft 1in), Height 2.92m (9ft 7in)
Powerplant: One 620kW (830hp) Bristol Mercury VIII 9 cylinder air-cooled radial piston engine

Maximum speed: 460km/h (290mph)
Range: 930km (580 miles)
Ceiling: 11,350m (37,240ft)
Crew: 1
Armament: Four 7.7mm (0.303in) Vickers machine guns in wings

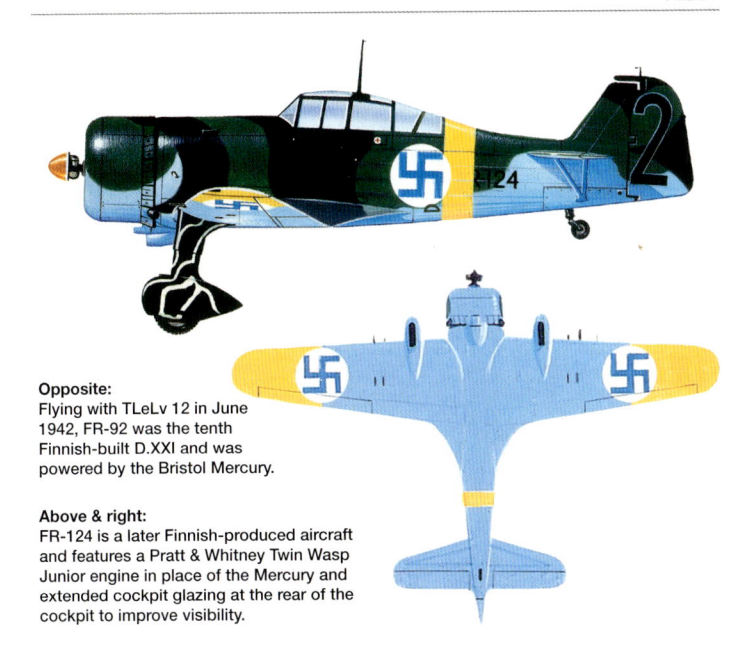

Opposite:
Flying with TLeLv 12 in June 1942, FR-92 was the tenth Finnish-built D.XXI and was powered by the Bristol Mercury.

Above & right:
FR-124 is a later Finnish-produced aircraft and features a Pratt & Whitney Twin Wasp Junior engine in place of the Mercury and extended cockpit glazing at the rear of the cockpit to improve visibility.

licence and built 93 more aircraft. D.XXIs were also manufactured in Republican Spain, though none was completed before the Nationalists overran the factory, and in Denmark, where 10 were produced.

Winter war

The first nation to take the Fokker into action was Finland during the Winter War against the Soviet Union of 1939–40. The D.XXI was the main Finnish fighter type during the conflict and proved successful, being credited with 130 victories while suffering 12 losses. Finnish D.XXIs remained operational during the Continuation War of 1941–44 but the aircraft, while still fairly effective, was by this point outclassed by modern Soviet types. Relegated to the training role, the last Finnish example was retired in 1949. In Dutch service, the D.XXI proved surprisingly effective against the Bf 109E during the 'Five-Day War' with Germany, mainly due to its excellent manoeuvrability, and accounted for 16 confirmed victories.

Fokker G.1

> Radical and impressive, the G.1 was influential but saw only brief, intense action in 1940. Intended as a *Jachtkruiser* ('hunting cruiser'), the aircraft originated as a private venture.

One of the crop of 'heavy fighters' produced in various nations in the thirties, the G.1 caused a stir when it appeared at the Paris Air Show in 1936, before it had even flown, gaining the nickname *le Facheur* ('the Reaper') in reference to its heavy installed armament of eight machine guns, all mounted in the nose. The twin boom configuration was most unusual at the time and the G.1 elicited considerable

The prototype G.1 in flight. By the time this photograph was taken the aircraft had been re-engined with Pratt & Whitney Twin Wasps.

Fokker G.1

Weight: 5000kg (11,023lb)
Dimensions: Length 10.87m (35ft 8in), Wingspan 17.16m (56ft 4in), Height 3.8m (12ft 6in)
Powerplant: Two 540kW (730hp) Bristol Mercury VIII 9-cylinder air cooled radial piston
Maximum speed: 475km/h (295mph)
Range: 1510km (940 miles)

Ceiling: 10,000m (33,000ft)
Crew: 2 or 3
Armament: Eight 7.9mm (0.31in) forward-firing FN-Browning machine guns in the nose (two 23mm (0.9in) Madsen cannon could be optionally fitted in place of four of the machine guns) and one 7.9mm (0.31in) machine gun in rear turret; up to 300kg (660lb) of bombs

Opposite:
This illustration removes the portside wing and tailboom to reveal the fuselage pod. Clarence 'Kelly' Johnson stated that the G.1 inspired his Lockheed P-38 Lightning design.

Above:
The prototype as first flown with no national markings and powered by Hispano-Suiza 80-02 engines.

Above:
Most production G.1s were powered by the Bristol Mercury but 11 were fitted with Pratt & Whitney Twin Wasp Juniors including number 343 illustrated.

international interest. Orders were received from Denmark, Spain and Sweden, though in the event the German invasion of the Netherlands precluded any of these orders from being fulfilled.

Brief combat role

The aircraft flew for the first time on 16 March 1937 and 36 were ordered for the Netherlands LVA (*Luchtvaartafdeling*: 'Army Aviation Group') of which 23 were serviceable when Germany opened hostilities in May 1940, although several were immediately lost on the ground in the opening assault. The surviving aircraft were mainly employed in ground attack missions but were also used in air combat to attack Junkers Ju 52/3m transports and were credited with 14 air-to-air victories in the brief conflict. The Germans allowed completion of those aircraft on the production line, utilizing these and surviving LVA G.1s as trainers for Bf 110 crews.

PZL P.11

Although past its prime by 1939, a PZL.11c attained the first Allied air-to-air victory on the first day of the war, shooting down a Ju 87 *Stuka*.

PZL had produced a series of gull-wing monoplane fighters of ever-better performance, starting with the P.1 of 1929. The P.11 had flown for the first time in August 1934, derived from the similar P.7, which would itself see combat in small numbers during 1939, but fitted with a more powerful engine and demonstrating considerably better performance as a result. When it entered service in late

A PZL P.11f of the Rumanian Air Force parked next to IAR 80s during the Balkans campaign, April 1941.

PZL P.11c

Weight: 1800kg (3968lb)
Dimensions: Length 7.55m (24ft 9in), Wingspan 10.72m (35ft 2in), Height 2.85m (9ft 4in)
Powerplant: One 420kW (560hp) Bristol Mercury V.S2 9-cylinder air-cooled radial piston engine
Maximum speed: 390km/h (240mph)

Range: 700km (430 miles)
Ceiling: 8000m (26,000ft)
Crew: 1
Armament: Two 7.92mm (0.312in) wz. 33 machine guns in fuselage and two optional 7.92mm (0.312in) wz. 33 machine guns in wings

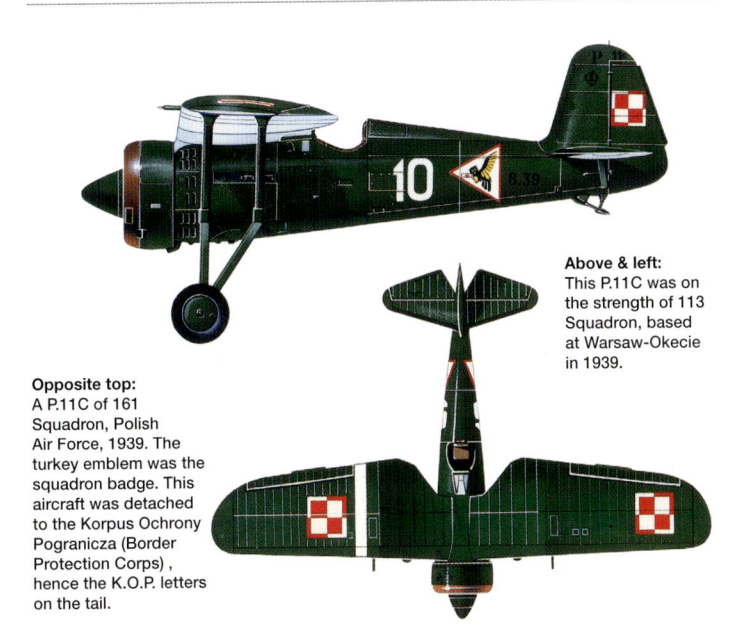

Above & left:
This P.11C was on the strength of 113 Squadron, based at Warsaw-Okecie in 1939.

Opposite top:
A P.11C of 161 Squadron, Polish Air Force, 1939. The turkey emblem was the squadron badge. This aircraft was detached to the Korpus Ochrony Pogranicza (Border Protection Corps) , hence the K.O.P. letters on the tail.

1934, the P.11 was arguably the best fighter in the world but such was the pace of military aircraft development that five years later it was essentially obsolete. Unfortunately for the Polish, the P.11's intended replacement, the PZL.50 *Jastrząb* ('Hawk'), was delayed and only the prototype had flown when Germany invaded in September 1939.

Outgunned

Not only was the P.11 slower than the Bf 109 fighter (and indeed most bombers), the German fighter also possessed greater firepower, though the P.11 was much more manoeuvrable and was a very strong aircraft. Despite its comparatively poor performance, P.11s shot down around 110 German aircraft in the month-long campaign, losing around 100 of their own. In addition to its Polish use, the P.11 was supplied to Romania where the aircraft was also produced under licence by IAR. Romanian P.11s were used in the opening stages of the invasion of the USSR.

PZL P.24

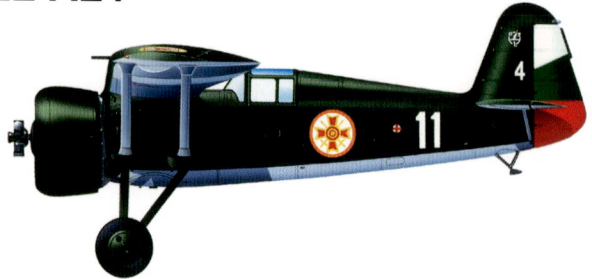

Produced solely for export, the PZL P.24 never served with its country of origin, but saw considerable action with Greece and Romania.

Derived from the P.11, the P.24 was designed specifically with the export market in mind. The engine was changed from the Bristol Mercury to the Gnome-Rhône 14K and the first prototype flew during May 1934. The third prototype set a world speed record for radial engine fighters when it achieved 414km/h (257mph) in June. The aircraft attracted considerable attention and aircraft were

The second P.24 prototype was photographed on a Greek airfield during its marketing tour of Bulgaria, Greece, Hungary and Turkey.

PZL P.24F

Weight: 2000kg (4409lb)
Dimensions: Length 7.5m (24ft 7in), Wingspan 10.72m (35ft 2in), Height 2.69m (8ft 10in)
Powerplant: One 720kW (970hp) Gnome-Rhône 14N-07 14-cylinder air-cooled radial piston engine
Maximum speed: 434km/h (267mph)
Range: 700km (430 miles)

Ceiling: 9000m (30,000ft)
Crew: 1
Armament: Two Oerlikon FF 20mm (0.79in) cannon and two Colt–Browning 7.7mm (0.303in) MG40 machine guns in wings, later four MG40 machine guns in wings; up to 100kg (220lb) bombload underwings

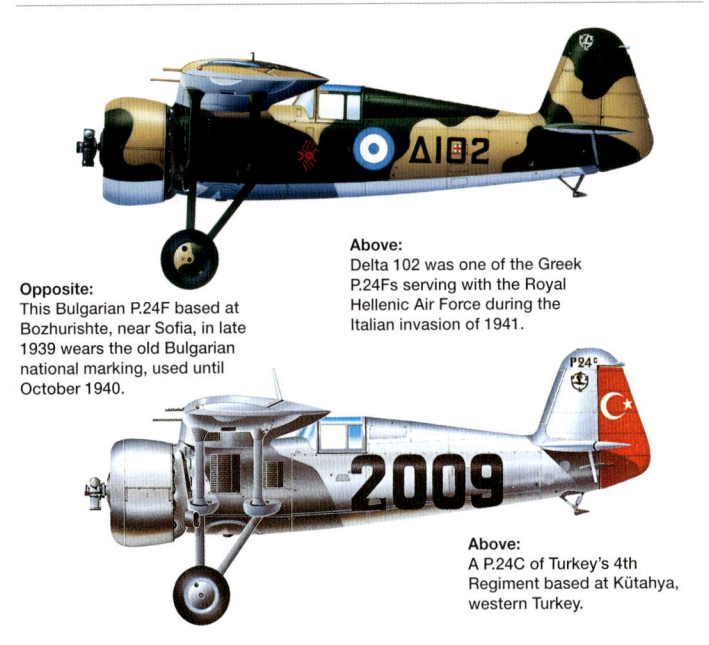

Opposite:
This Bulgarian P.24F based at Bozhurishte, near Sofia, in late 1939 wears the old Bulgarian national marking, used until October 1940.

Above:
Delta 102 was one of the Greek P.24Fs serving with the Royal Hellenic Air Force during the Italian invasion of 1941.

Above:
A P.24C of Turkey's 4th Regiment based at Kütahya, western Turkey.

subsequently supplied to Bulgaria, Greece, Romania and Turkey. Other nations had placed orders for improved variants by 1939 but the German occupation precluded any further export sales and Bulgaria in particular suffered with spare parts supply issues and made comparatively little use of their P.24s.

Greek service

By contrast, the P.24 was the main fighter type of Greece when Italy invaded in 1940 and engaged in heavy fighting. The P.24 was slightly slower than its primary fighter opponent, the Fiat CR.42, and the Italian machine was more manoeuvrable. However, the P.24 possessed significantly heavier firepower with twin 20mm (0.79in) cannon, at least until the ammunition supply ran out, forcing the aircraft to be re-armed with four 7.7mm (0.303in) machine guns. Ultimately Greek P.24s destroyed 64 aircraft for the loss of 24 PZLs in action. Romanian P.24s were used to defend the Ploiesti oilfields and Bucharest and were credited with 37 Soviet bombers destroyed before their replacement in 1942.

Lavochkin LaGG-3

An unpopular aircraft, the LaGG-3 was overweight, underpowered and prone to some unpleasant handling characteristics. Despite its shortcomings it was built in large numbers.

Designed as a replacement for the I-16 by Semyon Lavochkin, Vladimir Gorbunov and Mikhail Gudkov (the odd 'LaGG' designation being a portmanteau of their surnames' initial letters), the LaGG-3 was intended as a general purpose 'frontal fighter'. The design found ready favour due to its largely wooden construction, bypassing steel and alloy shortages prevailing in the USSR. The prototype,

In typically harsh conditions, a LaGG-3 of the 3rd Guards Fighter Aviation Regiment (GVIAP) prepares for a mission over Lake Ladoga, Karelia in 1943.

Lavochkin LaGG-3 66 Series

Weight: (maximum take-off): 3190kg (7033lb)
Dimensions: Length 8.81m (28ft 11in), Wingspan 9.8m (32ft 2in), Height 2.54m (8ft 4in)
Powerplant: One 924kW (1239hp) Klimov M-105PF V-12 liquid-cooled piston engine

Speed: 589km/h (366mph)
Range: 1000km (620 miles)
Ceiling: 9700m (31,800ft)
Crew: 1
Armament: One 12.7mm (0.5in) Berezin BS machine gun, one 20mm (0.79in) ShVAK cannon, two 50kg (110lb) bombs or six RS-82 or RS-132 rockets

Opposite:
'White 57' was forced down
by Finnish pilot Altto Tervo
in September 1942. It was
subsequently repaired and served
with the Finns as 'LG-3'.

Above (both images):
This LaGG-3 of 524 Fighter Aviation
Regiment (IAP) was shot down by
Finnish ground fire in March 1942.
Repaired, it entered Finnish service
as 'LG-1' and shot down a Soviet
LaGG-3 on 16 February 1944.

designated LaGG-1, made its maiden flight on 30 March 1940 but rate of
climb was poor and the handling so bad that an urgent programme of weight
reduction was undertaken. In modified form the aircraft entered production as
the LaGG-3 but was still liable to develop a violent spin without warning in a
steep turn and would stall at the slightest provocation.

Shortcomings

Although it was an extremely sturdy aircraft, the undercarriage was weak,
visibility from the cockpit was poor and initial build quality was dreadful. Many
of its worst issues were greatly improved over the course of production but the
LaGG-3 was always regarded as inferior to the Bf 109 and Fw 190 by friend and
foe alike. Despite its problems some pilots did achieve considerable success
with the LaGG and the top scorer is believed to have been Andrei Kulagin who
shot down 26 aircraft. Production ceased in 1944 after 6528 had been built and
the aircraft remained in service until the end of the war.

Lavochkin La-5

A change of engine utterly transformed the disappointing LaGG-3 into the successful La-5 that possessed excellent handling characteristics and performance.

To safeguard against potential production shortages of inline engines, the adaptation of existing inline-engined Soviet fighter aircraft to radial engines was undertaken from the summer of 1941. Accordingly work went ahead to adapt the LaGG-3 to the Shvetsov M-82, though this engine was quarter of a tonne heavier than the Klimov it replaced and adapting the slender fuselage

The short intake trunking atop the cowling reveals this to be an La-5F with the M-82F engine.

Lavochkin La-5FN

Weight: 3402kg (7500lb)
Dimensions: Length 8.67m (28ft 5in), Wingspan 9.8m (32ft 2in), Height 2.54m (8ft 4in)
Powerplant One 1380kW (1850hp) Shvetsov M-82FN 14-cylinder air-cooled radial engine
Speed: 648km/h (403mph)

Range: 765km (475 miles)
Ceiling: 11,000m (36,000ft)
Crew: 1
Armament: Two 20mm (0.79in) ShVAK cannon; two bombs up to 100kg (220lb) each

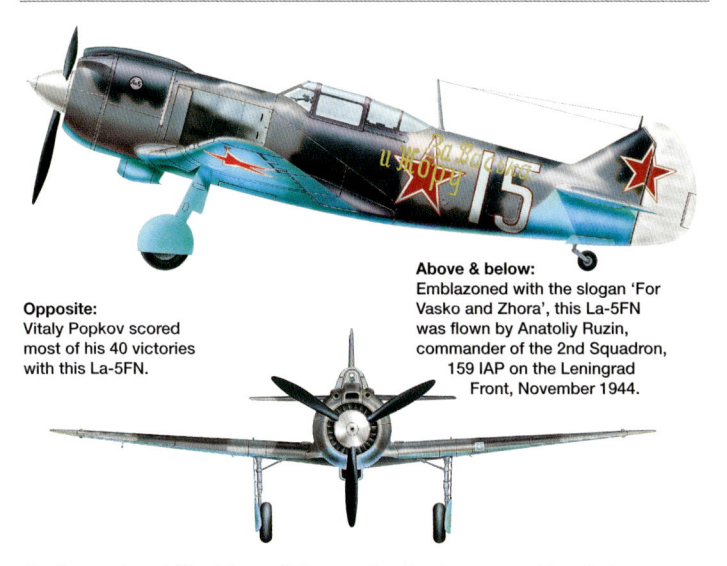

Opposite:
Vitaly Popkov scored most of his 40 victories with this La-5FN.

Above & below:
Emblazoned with the slogan 'For Vasko and Zhora', this La-5FN was flown by Anatoliy Ruzin, commander of the 2nd Squadron, 159 IAP on the Leningrad Front, November 1944.

for the greater width of the radial was not a simple process. Nonetheless the conversion was completed in December 1941 and flight testing revealed such an improvement in performance that a priority directive was issued that all existing LaGG-3 airframes in production should be converted to the M-82 immediately. Committed to action from September 1942 over Stalingrad, the new fighter proved excellent, retaining the immense strength of the LaGG-3 but demonstrating greater speed, rate of climb and manoeuvrability.

La-5FN

Initial production aircraft utilized a fuselage largely unchanged from the LaGG-3 but the La-5 soon received a cut-down rear fuselage to improve visibility and from late 1942 the M-82F 'boosted' engine offered an increase in power, followed in early 1943 by the even more potent M-82FN 'directly boosted' engine which featured fuel injection. This powered the definitive La-5FN that began to appear in numbers over the front during March 1943. During this period Ivan Kozhedub, the most successful Allied fighter pilot of all, who would score most of his 62 victories with the La-5FN, began his dramatic rise to prominence.

Lavochkin La-7

Taking the development of the La-5 to its wartime zenith, the La-7 was an outstanding fighter and the last fighter of predominantly wooden construction to see widespread service.

Developed from the La-5FN, the La-7 is easily distinguished from the earlier aircraft by the removal of the prominent supercharger air intake above the cowling, the intake moving to the port wing root. First flown in November 1943, the La-7 began to reach the front as early as the late spring of 1944, offering a useful improvement to the performance and handling. The new aircraft retained

Lavochkin La 7 'White 10', from a guards regiment on the Baltic Front, 1944.

Lavochkin La-7

Weight: 3400kg (7496lb)
Dimensions: Length 8.6m (28ft 3in), Wingspan 9.8m (32ft 2in), Height 2.54m (8ft 4in)
Powerplant: 1380kW (1850hp) Shvetsov M-82FN 14-cylinder air-cooled radial engine
Speed: 661km/h (411mph)

Range: 665km (413 miles)
Ceiling: 10,450m (34,280ft)
Crew: 1
Armament: Two cowl-mounted 20mm (0.79in) ShVAK cannons or three 20mm (0.79in) Berezin B-20 cannons; up to 200kg (440lb) bombload

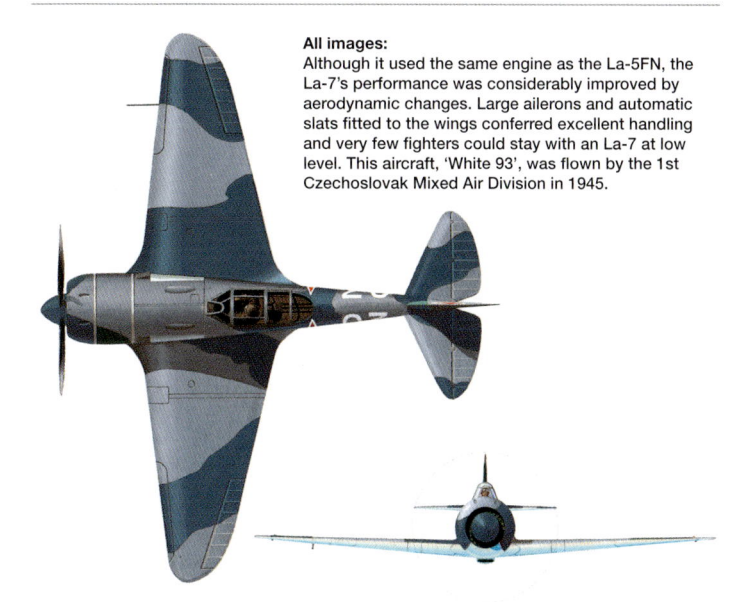

All images:
Although it used the same engine as the La-5FN, the La-7's performance was considerably improved by aerodynamic changes. Large ailerons and automatic slats fitted to the wings conferred excellent handling and very few fighters could stay with an La-7 at low level. This aircraft, 'White 93', was flown by the 1st Czechoslovak Mixed Air Division in 1945.

the exemplary handling of the earlier Lavochkin fighter and its dog-fighting capability at low altitude was regarded as superior to any contemporary fighter. In combat the La-7 proved formidable, and although it featured the capability to carry bombs for ground attack work, it was almost exclusively used in the air superiority role.

Up-armed

Initially armed with two 20mm (0.79in) ShVAK cannon, identical to the La-5FN, this armament was regarded as inadequate against contemporary German aircraft and a new arrangement with three 20mm (0.79in) Berezin B-20 cannon mounted asymmetrically in the fuselage nose, two to port and one to starboard, was tested during 1944. Offering a significantly heavier weight of fire, the three-gun version went into production in January 1945. Despite its excellent performance, the La-7 was always regarded as an interim model pending delivery of the all-metal La-9, but the latter aircraft only flew in 1946 and the La-7 remained the ultimate Lavochkin fighter to see combat in World War II.

Mikoyan Gurevich MiG-3

Intended for high-altitude interceptions, the nature of air combat on the Eastern Front saw the MiG-3 utilized at lower altitudes than was intended and its effectiveness suffered.

First flown on 5 April 1940, the small but heavy I-200 demonstrated excellent speed at high altitude, but longitudinal stability was poor and control response sluggish. It would fall easily into a vicious spin and landing characteristics were so bad it was recommended that only the most experienced pilots fly the aircraft. Despite this, an initial batch of 100 aircraft, designated MiG-1,

MiG-3s pictured in winter camouflage during the defence of Moscow. The nearest aircraft features the slogan 'For the Motherland'.

Mikoyan Gurevich MiG-3

Weight: 3355kg (7397lb)
Dimensions: Length 8.25m (27ft 1in), Wingspan 10.2m (33ft 6in), Height 3.3m (10ft 10in)
Powerplant: One 1007kW (1350hp) Mikulin AM-35A V-12 liquid-cooled piston engine
Speed: 640km/h (400mph)

Range: 820km (510 miles)
Ceiling: 12,000m (39,000ft)
Crew: 1
Armament: One 12.7mm (0.5in) Berezin UBS machine gun, two 7.62mm (0.3in) ShKAS machine guns

Above:
'White 04' was flown by Sergey
Polyakov in the defence of
Leningrad in mid 1941.

Opposite top:
In temporary winter camouflage,
'Red 36' was operating with the 12
GvIAP in the defence of Moscow
during the winter of 1941–42.

Above:
This MiG-3 served with 7 IAP
(aviation regiment) in 1943.

was ordered in May 1940 and work progressed to remedy the worst of the
faults, resulting in the MiG-3. The wing was given increased dihedral to improve
lateral stability and the engine moved forward 100mm (4in) which did little for
forward visibility but significantly improved longitudinal stability. The MiG-3 was
still an aircraft with difficult handling but the urgent need for modern fighters
outweighed such concerns and large-scale production began in February 1941.

First combat

Once committed to combat the MiG-3 was found wanting, for although faster
than the Bf 109F at high altitude, virtually all combat took place at lower
altitudes where the MiG-3 possessed no speed advantage. The aircraft also
possessed a loaded weight some 220kg (485lb) greater than the Messerschmitt
and was less manoeuvrable, resulting in heavy losses. Despite its flaws, a few
talented pilots were able to achieve good results with the MiG-3 but production
ended in late 1941 and the aircraft redeployed from the front to defend cities
and strategic targets, a role in which the MiG proved competent, remaining in
service for several years.

Petlyakov Pe-3

Nocturnal raids on Moscow began in July 1941 and an urgent programme commenced to field a suitable night fighter resulting in the development of the Pe-3, derived from the Pe-2 bomber.

The Pe-2 bomber had itself started life as a fighter so its development came full circle when the Pe-3 fighter derivative appeared. The Pe-3 featured the bare minimum of changes required to allow it to operate in its new role and the urgency attached to its production can be judged by the fact that the initial conversion was ordered to be completed in a mere four days. Subsequent production

Few bombers make good fighters but the Pe-2, from which the Pe-3 derived, was famed for its outstanding performance. These are Pe-2FTs over the Baltic coast.

Petlyakov Pe-3

Weight: 8000kg (17,637lb)
Dimensions: Length 12.66m (41ft 6in), Wingspan 17.13m (56ft 2in), Height 3.5m (11ft 6in)
Powerplant: Two 820kW (1100hp) Klimov M-105RA V-12 liquid-cooled piston engines
Speed: 530km/h (330mph)
Range: 500km (930 miles)

Ceiling: 9100m (29,900ft)
Crew: 2
Armament: One 20mm (0.79in) ShVAK cannon in the nose, two 12.7mm (0.5in) UBK machine guns in the fuselage, one 12.7mm (0.5in) UBT machine gun in dorsal turret, one 7.62mm (0.3in) ShKAS machine gun fixed firing rearward in tail cone); 700kg (1543lb) bombload

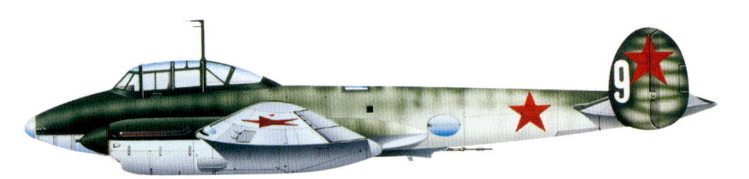

Opposite & above:
The Petlyakov Pe-2 was an outstanding tactical
attack aircraft from which the Pe-3 was developed.

Above:
With its field-applied temporary white camouflage,
this Pe-3 operated with 6 IAK of the Moscow Air
Defence Forces (PVO) during the winter of 1941–42.

of the Pe-3 began before proper drawings had been prepared and workers
fabricated parts based on sketches and adjusted them to fit by hand. The
Pe-3 could be easily distinguished from the Pe-2 by its lack of nose glazing,
replaced by fittings for two 12.7mm (0.5in) UBK machine guns. Slats to improve
manoeuvrability took the place of the Pe-2's dive brakes and the bomb bay was
used for fuel. The ventral gun position was deleted to allow greater fuel capacity
but the dorsal 7.62mm (0.3in) was retained along with the small bomb bays at
the rear of the engine nacelles.

Up-armed model

Combat experience revealed a need for armour protection and increased
firepower resulting in the Pe-3bis which added a ShVAK 20mm (0.79in) cannon
in the nose as well as armour. In service the 360 Pe-3s constructed operated
as night fighters and ground attack aircraft but ultimately the Pe-3's speed and
range saw it used instead for reconnaissance, a role it performed until the end
of hostilities.

Polikarpov I-15

The highly manoeuvrable I-15 had proved effective during the Spanish Civil War but by the time of the German invasion it was long overdue for replacement.

The barrel-shaped I-15 first flew in 1933, demonstrating outstanding manoeuvrability and climb. Powered by an American Wright R-1820 Cyclone engine, which Shvetsov would produce under licence as the M-25 (though all early I-15s were powered by imported engines), the I-15 entered service in 1934 and proved popular with pilots. Subsequently, reservations about

Polikarpov's biplane fighters enjoyed a successful second career as ground attack aircraft.

Polikarpov I-15

Weight: 1689kg (3724lb)
Dimensions: Length 6.10m (20ft 0in), Wingspan 9.75m (32ft 0in), Height 2.20m (7ft 3in)
Powerplant: One 520kW (700hp) Shvetsov M-25 9-cylinder air-cooled radial engine

Speed: 367km/h (228mph)
Range: 510km (320 miles)
Ceiling: 9800m (32,200ft)
Crew: 1
Armament: Four 7.62mm (0.3in) PV-1 machine guns; up to 50kg (110lb) bombload

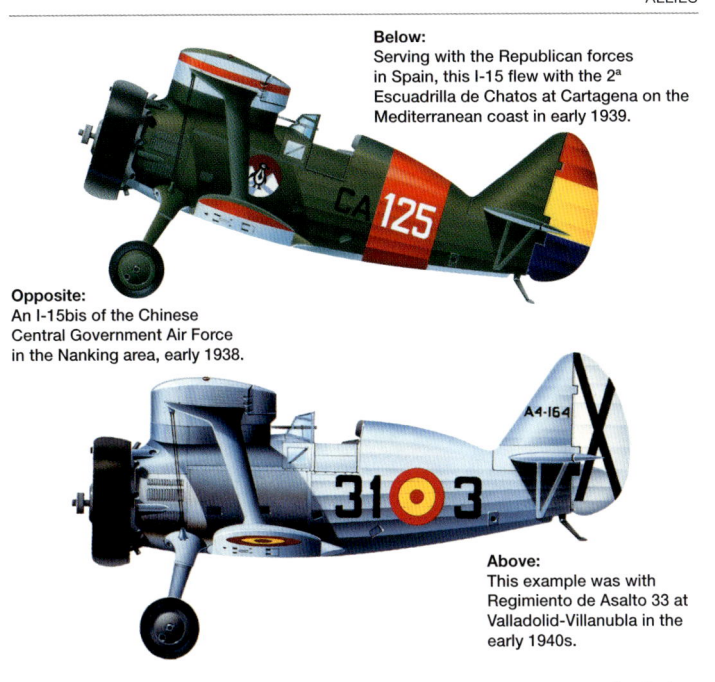

Below:
Serving with the Republican forces in Spain, this I-15 flew with the 2ª Escuadrilla de Chatos at Cartagena on the Mediterranean coast in early 1939.

Opposite:
An I-15bis of the Chinese Central Government Air Force in the Nanking area, early 1938.

Above:
This example was with Regimiento de Asalto 33 at Valladolid-Villanubla in the early 1940s.

the lack of visibility afforded by the gulled arrangement of the upper wing led to the development of the I-15bis with conventional cabane struts. Possessing essentially identical performance, the I-15bis entered production in 1937 by which time the I-15 had seen extensive operational service in Spain where it had proved markedly superior to the Heinkel He 51 and roughly equivalent in capability to the Fiat CR.32.

However, as more advanced monoplane fighters appeared, the I-15 was increasingly sidelined. After seeing action against the Finnish and Japanese, by June 1941 around 1000 I-15 and I-15bis, now totally obsolete, remained in frontline service and the I-15 suffered heavy losses in air combat against the Germans, though its agility could still cause problems for opposing fighters. The aircraft enjoyed some success as a close support aircraft despite only carrying a modest 50kg (110lb) bombload or up to six RS-82 rockets, but by the end of 1942, all surviving I-15s were operating in secondary roles.

Polikarpov I-153

Although probably the finest biplane fighter ever built, the supremely agile I-153 was conceptually obsolete by the opening of World War II.

The I-153 owed its existence to experience garnered during combat with the nimble Fiat CR.32 in Spain that convinced Soviet planners to continue developing agile biplane fighters. The retractable undercarriage I-153 was intended to deliver the highest possible performance without sacrificing the manoeuvrability of the biplane configuration. First flown in August 1938, the I-153 reverted to

This I-153 was downed near Kerimäki in June 1941 and was subsequently repaired and used by the Finnish Air Force, coded VH-19.

Polikarpov I-153

Weight: 2110kg (4652lb)
Dimensions: Length 6.17m (20ft 3in),
Wingspan 10m (32ft 10in), Height 2.8m (9ft 2in)
Powerplant: One 597kW (801hp) Shvetsov
M-62 9-cylinder air-cooled radial piston engine
Speed: 297km/h (185mph)

Range: 470km (290 miles)
Ceiling: 10,700m (35,100ft)
Crew: 1
Armament: Four 7.62mm (0.3in) ShKAS
machine guns; eight RS-82 rockets

Right:
Flown by Konstantin Solovyov of 71 IAP, this I-153 was based at Suomenlahti in Finland.

Opposite top:
'Black 69' ws flying with 148 IAP when it was captured near Liepaja in Latvia after a forced landing in the opening weeks of Operation Barbarossa in 1941.

Above:
'White 19' was roughly painted green over its original silver finish while serving on the Karelian Front during the autumn of 1941.

the gull-wing centre section of the I-15, rather than the cabane of the I-15bis, to minimize drag, inspiring its *Chaika* ('Seagull') nickname. Soon after entering service, the I-153 was fighting in the Battles of Khalkhin Gol, after the I-16 was found to be struggling to cope with the agile Nakajima Ki 27, and I-153s were rushed to the front specifically to deal with the Japanese fighter.

The two aircraft were closely matched and the success of the I-153 in this theatre appeared to vindicate the decision to produce a modern biplane fighter. During the Winter War with Finland the I-153 performed adequately but come 1941, the obsolescent I-153 biplane stood little chance against the Bf 109. Comprising nearly half the front line fighter inventory when Operation Barbarossa was launched, the I-153 suffered tremendous losses, though its outstanding manoeuvrability could cause problems if well handled and some Soviet pilots managed to score a few victories with the type. Switched to close support duties, the I-153 soldiered on until mid 1943, though the Finns operated captured I-153s until the end of hostilities.

Polikarpov I-16

Though largely unknown in the West at the time, the stubby Polikarpov I-16 was one of the most significant and groundbreaking combat aircraft in history

First flown on the last day of 1933, Nikolai Polikarpov's I-16 was tricky to fly but boasted a performance superior to any fighter then in service. It was the world's first cantilever monoplane fighter with enclosed cockpit and retractable undercarriage, though the latter feature required 44 turns of a handle in the cockpit to retract and the claustrophobic forward-sliding enclosed canopy

The I-16s of the Soviet display team, the 'Red Five'. These aircraft were finished, unsurprisingly, in overall red.

Polikarpov I-16 Type 24

Weight: 1941kg (4279lb)
Dimensions: Length 6.13m (20ft 1in), Wingspan 9m (29ft 6in), Height 3.25m (10ft 8in)
Powerplant: One 820kW (1100hp) Shvetsov M-63 9-cylinder air-cooled radial piston engine
Speed: 525km/h (326mph)
Range: 700km (430 miles)

Ceiling: 9700m (31,800ft)
Crew: 1
Armament: Two 7.62mm (0.3in) ShKAS machine guns in upper cowling, two 20mm (0.79in) ShVAK cannons in the wings; six unguided RS-82 rockets or up to 500kg (1100lb) of bombs

Opposite top:
This winter-camouflaged I-16 Type 24 was operating in the Lake Lagoda area, Leningrad, during the winter of 1940–41 with 4 GvIAP of the Baltic Fleet.

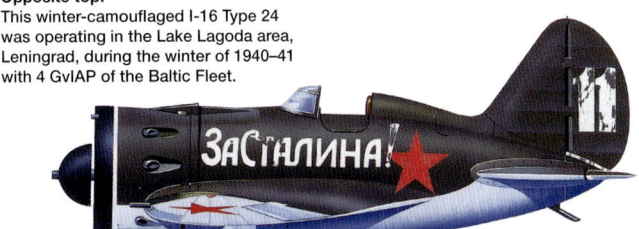

Above:
Ace Boris Safanov flew this I-16 over Murmansk in 1941. *Za Stalina!* translates as 'For Stalin!'

Below:
The 'Double Top' domino fin badge reveals this to be an I-16 Type 10 of the 3ª Escuadrilla de Moscas.

gradually became opaque when exposed to sunlight and was discarded in later production models. In Spain, Republican I-16s gained air superiority from the rebels, proving initially superior to all other fighters in the theatre. Combat experience revealed the firepower provided by just two 7.62mm (0.3in) ShKAS machine guns was inadequate and though two further such weapons were added, and later two 20mm (0.79in) cannon were fitted, by the time of the German assault the I-16 was obsolete, though it remained the most commonly encountered Soviet fighter until the end of 1942.

Outclassed

Against the Bf 109, the nimble I-16 was still competitive in the hands of a good pilot and many Soviet aces scored their first victories with it, but the German fighter was faster and better armed. By the end of 1943 the vast majority of I-16s were in second-line roles, though the last operational I-16 fighters, based in the far east of Russia, were exchanged for Bell Kingcobras as late as August 1945. Total production of all I-16 variants was 10,292.

Yakovlev Yak-1

> Built to the same requirement as the LaGG-3, the Yak-1 was Aleksandr Yakovlev's first fighter design and, in stark contrast to its competitor, was light and easy to handle.

Ordered into production around a month after the prototype's first flight on 13 January 1940, the Yak-1 was small, simple and of mixed wood and metal construction to minimize demand on strategic light alloy supplies. It was ideally suited to the conditions it would encounter on the Eastern Front but the aircraft had been committed to production prematurely and numerous problems

A row of Yak-1 fighters stand on an airfield somewhere in the Soviet Union, 1941.

Yakovlev Yak-1 (late production, typical)

Weight: 2884kg (6358lb)
Dimensions: Length 8.48m (27ft 10in), Wingspan 10.0m (32ft 10in), Height 2.64m (8ft 8in)
Powerplant: One 940kW (1260hp) Klimov M-105PF V-12 liquid-cooled piston engine
Speed: 592km/h (368mph)

Range: 700km (430 miles)
Ceiling: 10,050m (32,970ft)
Crew: 1
Armament: One 20mm (0.79in) ShVAK cannon and one 12.7mm (0.5in) Berezin UBS machine gun

Opposite:
After October 1942 Yak-1s were
built with a bubble canopy
and cut-down rear fuselage,
designated Yak-1M.

Above:
Serving with an unknown unit over central
Russia during 1941–42, this Yak-1 features
a temporary white scheme of water-
soluble paint.

Above:
Mikhail Baranov was the leading
Soviet ace of 1942, flying this Yak-1
marked with 27 victories.

had to be overcome as the aircraft began to roll off the line – 7460 changes were
implemented in the first four months of production alone. As a result, aircraft
were essentially hand-finished and Yak-1s ended up with bizarre problems such
as different length landing gear legs and parts that were not interchangeable
between aircraft, and no two aircraft could be relied upon to have the same
performance.

Best domestic fighter

Nonetheless, the Yak-1 was the best of the domestic fighter types that faced
the German assault in the summer of 1941. By 1942 it was a reliable aircraft
and popular with pilots, though with just one 20mm (0.79in) cannon and a pair
of machine guns it was not well armed. Later production saw the twin ShKAS
7.62mm (0.3in) guns replaced with a single 12.7mm (0.5in) Berezin UBS and
from October 1942 a cut-down rear fuselage and bubble canopy. An important
change was the introduction of the M-105PF 'boosted' engine which, mated to
a lightened airframe, resulted in a distinct improvement to performance.

Yakovlev Yak-3

The finest close-in dogfighter produced in the Soviet Union, the Yak-3 brought the wartime development of the basic Yak fighter to its zenith.

The Yak-3 started life as the lightened Yak-1M *Moskit* ('Mosquito'), intended to deliver the best possible air-to-air combat performance, with reduced span wings and aerodynamic improvements, the most externally obvious of which being the relocation of the oil cooler from under the nose to the wing roots. First flown in February 1943, the Yak-1M was tested against captured examples of the Fw-190A-4

'White 10' is an early production Yak-3. The Yak-3 was highly popular with pilots who nicknamed it *Ubiytsa* ('Killer').

Yakovlev Yak-3

Weight: 2697kg (5946lb)
Dimensions: Length 8.5m (27ft 11in), Wingspan 9.2m (30ft 2in), Height 2.64m (8ft 8in)
Powerplant: One 960kW (1290hp) Klimov VK-105PF2 V-12 liquid-cooled piston engine
Speed: 646km/h (401mph)

Range: 550km (340 miles)
Ceiling: 10,400m (34,100ft)
Crew: 1
Armament: One 20mm (0.79in) ShVAK cannon and two 12.7mm (0.5in) Berezin UBS machine guns

Below:
By April 1945 'Blue
24' was based in East
Prussia with the 7
GvIAP of the 303 IAD.

Opposite top:
Yak-3 'White 100' was
flying with 492 IAP
as the unit entered
Germany in early 1945
and featured a stylized
winged sword emblem
on the nose.

Right: These are the
Yak-3s of the Free
French Normandie-
Niemen regiment that
fought as part of the
Soviet Air Force from
late 1942 onwards.

and Bf-109G-2 and was found to possess better performance than either at low
and medium altitude. Test pilots were enthusiastic and the aircraft was rushed
into production as the Yak-3. Initial deliveries were slow, as each Yak-3 required
2.5 times as many man hours to complete as a Yak-1, mostly due to the care
required in producing a high-quality surface finish, but by the start of 1945, 735
Yak-3s were on strength.

Supreme flier

In combat, it was admitted by the *Luftwaffe* for the first time that a Soviet fighter
was superior to their own when a famous 1944 general directive advised pilots
to 'avoid combat below 5000m with Yakovlev fighters lacking an oil cooler under
the nose'. Later development centred on improving the armament, culminating
in the Yak-3P which featured three Berezin B-20 20mm (0.79in) cannon, two in
the nose and one firing through the airscrew hub, though this appeared too late
to see wartime service. The radical Yak-3RD was built with a rocket motor in the
tail to boost maximum speed but this did not enter production.

Yakovlev Yak-7

Developed, unusually for a fighter, from a trainer, the Yak-7 complemented the Yak-1 in service and was the basis for further development in the shape of the definitive Yak-9.

In 1939 Yakovlev designed a two-seat derivative of his Yak-1, intended primarily as an advanced trainer though able to take on fast courier and light transport duties when required. First flown in the late summer of 1940, designated Yak-7UTI, the two-seater possessed a wing of 25cm (10in) greater span, slightly larger tail surfaces and a second cockpit with full flight controls. The undercarriage

Pictured as it appeared in the autumn of 1942, 'Red 8' is a bubble-canopied late-production Yak-7B serving with 42 IAP.

Yakovlev Yak-7 (early production, typical)

Weight: 2935kg (6471lb)
Dimensions: Length 8.48m (27ft 10in), Wingspan 10m (32ft 10in), Height 2.75m (9ft 0in)
Powerplant: One 780kW (1050hp) Klimov M-105PA V-12 liquid-cooled piston engine
Speed: 495km/h (308mph)

Range: 643km (400 miles)
Ceiling: 9500m (31,200ft)
Crew: 1
Armament: One 20mm (0.79in) ShVAK cannon and two 12.7mm (0.5in) Berezin UBS machine guns

Opposite:
The hump-backed profile of the Yak-7 makes obvious its trainer origins. This example still carries the remains of its winter camouflage in the spring of 1943.

Above:
'Red 8' is the same aircraft as in the photograph opposite. Note the 'kill' markings on the fuselage scroll motif; it was highly unusual to record victories with swastikas in Soviet fighter units during the war.

Right: Yak-7 fighters built with funds donated by collective farmers of the Bashkir Republic line up on an airfield.

was simplified and strengthened and armament was reduced to a single ShKAS of 7.62mm (0.3in) in the nose. However, in August 1941 staff at Factory 301 decided to alter a Yak-7UTI into a single-seat fighter. The rear cockpit was faired over, armament was increased to one 20mm (0.79in) ShVAK and two 12.7mm (0.5in) Berezin UB guns in the nose, and the 'new' fighter gained racks for six rockets under each wing. Flight testing revealed the single-seat Yak-7 was superior to the Yak-1 while retaining the useful ability to carry a passenger.

First combat

Production was swiftly initiated and the first Yak-7s entered combat during December 1941. Later Yak-7s received the same cut-down rear fuselage as the Yak-1 and although most of the Yak-7s built were standard fighters, a small batch of 22 Yak-7-37s with a 37mm (1.5in) cannon firing through the propeller hub was built during August 1942. By 1943 major structural changes, particularly to the wing, prompted a designation change to Yak-9.

Yakovlev Yak-9

The Yak-9 was the most numerous and versatile of the Yak fighter derivatives, appearing in a variety of specialized subtypes as well as the standard frontal fighter.

Two 'heavyweight' and 'lightweight' lines emerged in Yak development, though the terms were relative: compared with contemporary fighters, Yaks were *all* lightweight. The Yak-9 represented the culmination of the 'heavy' version. First appearing at the front during late November 1942, the Yak-9 differed from the Yak-7 primarily in its wings, which were now mostly constructed of light alloy, and

These Yak-9s bear the inscription of the donor, 'Little Theatre: Front'.

Yakovlev Yak-9D

Weight: 3080kg (6790lb)
Dimensions: Length 8.55m (28ft 0in), Wingspan 9.74m (31ft 11in), Height 2.75m (9ft 0in)
Powerplant: One 1014kW (1360hp) Klimov M-105PF-3 V-12 liquid-cooled piston engine
Speed: 602km/h (374mph)

Range: 1400km (870 miles)
Ceiling: 11,100m (36,400ft)
Crew: 1
Armament: One 20mm (0.79in) ShVAK cannon and one 12.7mm (0.5in) Berezin UBS machine gun

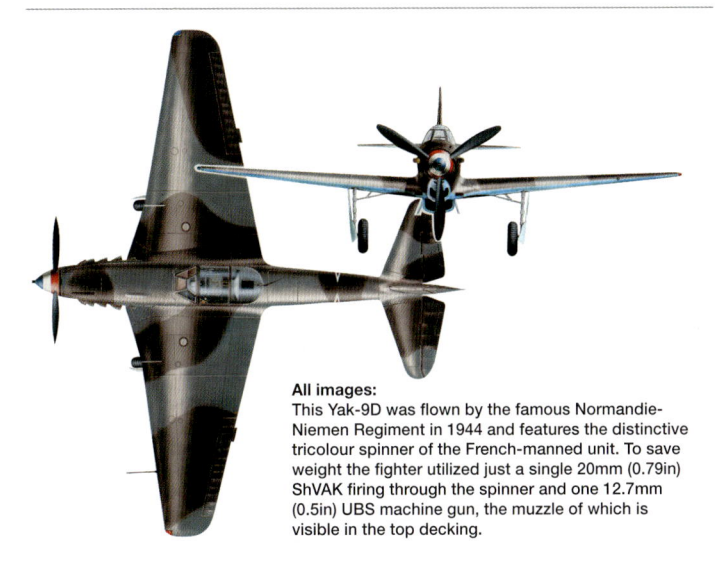

All images:
This Yak-9D was flown by the famous Normandie-Niemen Regiment in 1944 and features the distinctive tricolour spinner of the French-manned unit. To save weight the fighter utilized just a single 20mm (0.79in) ShVAK firing through the spinner and one 12.7mm (0.5in) UBS machine gun, the muzzle of which is visible in the top decking.

contained a greater fuel capacity. Longer-range versions were also developed: the Yak-9D *Dal'ny* 'Long' (range) boasted an internal capacity of 650 litres (170 gallons), increasing range to 1400km (870 miles). Later, the Yak-9DD *Dal'ny Deistviye* 'Ultra Long' increased this to a maximum of 2300km (1429 miles) and escorted USAAF B-17s and B-24s on shuttle bombing raids in the summer of 1944. The Yak-9B *Bombardirovshchik* squeezed four 100kg (220lb) bombs, nose-up, directly behind the cockpit and was intended for use against heavily defended targets but disappointed due to difficulties in bomb aiming and poor handling.

Heavy cannon

The contemporary Yak-9T *Tyazhely* 'Heavy' (cannon) mounted an NS-37 37mm (1.5in) cannon in the propeller hub, used to devastating effect against tanks and shipping. A version fitted with an even larger 45mm (1.8in) NS-45 cannon with distinctive muzzle brake was developed as a bomber destroyer but saw little use. Later development resulted in the Yak-9U, featuring the Klimov VK-107 engine which attained 700km/h (435mph) in testing. Teething issues with this engine meant that only a handful of these exceptional fighters made it into service before the ending of hostilities.

Blackburn Skua and Roc

The Skua boasted only modest performance but nonetheless became the first British aircraft to attack and shoot down an enemy aircraft in World War II.

The first British carrier monoplane to enter service, as well as being the first with retractable undercarriage, the Skua was expected to fulfil both the fighter and dive bomber role for the Fleet Air Arm. Flying for the first time on 9 February 1937, only 190 examples were built but were very heavily employed during the first two years of the war. On 26 September 1939, Skuas from HMS *Ark Royal*

The British Blackburn Roc included four 7.7mm (0.303in) Browning machine guns in a power-operated dorsal turret.

Blackburn Skua Mk II

Weight: 3732kg (8228lb)
Dimensions: Length 10.85m (35ft 7in), Wingspan 14.07m (46ft 2in), Height 3.81m (12ft 6in)
Powerplant: One 660kW (890hp) Bristol Perseus XII 9-cylinder air-cooled radial piston engine
Maximum speed: 362km/h (225mph)

Range: 1220km (760 miles)
Ceiling: 6200m (20,200ft)
Crew: 2
Armament: Four 7.7mm (0.303in) Browning machine guns fixed firing forward in wings, one 7.7mm (0.303in) Vickers K or Lewis machine gun flexibly mounted in rear cockpit; up to 227kg (500lb) bombload under fuselage

Opposite:
Although not a particularly good fighter, the Skua was an outstanding dive bomber. L2987 was serving aboard HMS *Ark Royal* in June 1940.

Above:
Only a few Rocs saw operational service, one of which was L3075 of No. 806 NAS which flew patrols and ground attack sorties over the Dunkirk evacuation beaches.

Right: Blackburn Skua Mk IIs of 803 Squadron in formation over the English coast, 1939.

intercepted three Dornier Do 18 flying boats and shot down one of them, the first successful air-to-air attack by a British aircraft (though the first British air-to-air victory of all was a Bf 109 downed by the gunner of a Fairey Battle fighter it was itself attacking). Although it proved an excellent dive bomber, the effectiveness of the Skua as a fighter was compromised by the assumption that it would rarely meet enemy fighters in combat and usually only have to deal with bombers and patrol aircraft and thus it was no match for enemy single-seaters. Nonetheless, despite its less than stellar performance, pilot William Lucy became the first Royal Navy 'ace', scoring all of his victories with the Skua.

Blackburn Roc
A turret fighter derivative of the Skua, the Roc, was slower and conceptually flawed but nonetheless managed to attain one victory in its short career. Both types had been withdrawn to second-line roles by early 1941.

Bristol Beaufighter

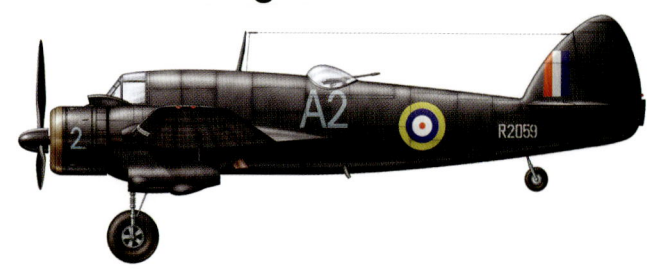

Developed at great speed from the Beaufort torpedo bomber, the Beaufighter became one of the most successful, and versatile, aircraft of the conflict.

The Beaufighter owed its existence to delays in the Typhoon and Whirlwind programmes and with the RAF keen to introduce a cannon-armed fighter, Bristol proposed a re-engined fighter version of the Beaufort which subsequently emerged as the Beaufighter, making its maiden flight in July 1939. From the outset the Beaufighter was armed with four 20mm (0.79in) Hispano cannon in

This Beaufighter Mk IF flew with No. 252 Squadron which became the first to take the aircraft overseas when they sent a detachment to Malta.

Bristol Beaufighter Mk IF

Weight: 9435kg (21,000lb)
Dimensions: Length 12.6m (41ft 4in), Wingspan 17.63m (57ft 10in), Height 4.82m (15ft 10in)
Powerplant: Two 1163kW (1560hp) Bristol Hercules XI 14-cylinder air-cooled radial piston engines
Maximum speed: 520km/h (323mph)

Range: 1883km (1170 miles)
Ceiling: 8077m (26,500ft)
Crew: 2
Armament: Four 20mm (0.79in) Hispano cannon fixed firing forward in nose and six 7.7mm (0.303in) Browning machine guns fixed firing forward in wings, four in starboard wing and two in port wing

Above:
This aircraft, finished in the standard RAF day fighter scheme applied to the first production Beaufighters, was taken on strength by No. 25 Squadron, based at North Weald in Kent in September 1940.

Opposite top:
Beaufighter R2059 made the first operational sortie of the type on 5 September 1940 before the Beaufighter entered regular squadron service later the same month.

Above:
Flown by the 415th Night Fighter Squadron of the USAAF in September 1943, this NF Mk VI was based at Gerbini in Sicily.

the lower front fuselage, supplemented by six 7.7mm (0.303in) machine guns, making the Beaufighter the most heavily armed British fighter of the war. Night fighting was initially the most important role for the Beaufighter and the first nocturnal victory was achieved on 25 October 1940. Improvements to both ground-based and airborne radar led to the Beaufighter's best night when 14 Luftwaffe bombers were shot down on the night of 10/11 May 1941.

Coastal command
Beaufighters also saw use by day with Coastal Command on anti-shipping duties until the end of the war and in the Western Desert, destroying 44 enemy aircraft on the ground and in the air in just four days during the 'Crusader' offensive of 1941. The USAAF also utilized the Beaufighter as a night fighter and the aircraft was licence-built in Australia, primarily for anti-shipping use. In terms of total numbers of aircraft shot down, the Beaufighter was the third most successful British aircraft after the Spitfire and the Hurricane.

Bristol Blenheim

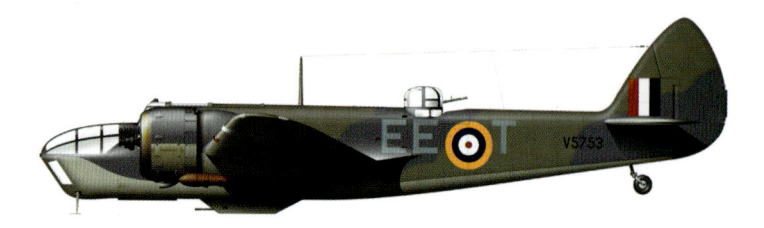

> **The Bristol Blenheim achieved the world's first air-to-air interception assisted by airborne radar but it was rapidly sidelined by later, higher-performance aircraft.**

In 1937 the Blenheim bomber entered service and its excellent performance by the standards of the day encouraged the development of a fighter version, the Blenheim Mk IF, which entered service in 1938. All fighter Blenheims were converted from standard bombers by simply adding a self-contained ventral gun pack containing four Browning machine guns. After the outbreak of

A head-on view of a Blenheim IF, the long-range heavy fighter version, armed with four 7.7mm (0.303in) machine guns.

Bristol Blenheim Mk IF

Weight: 5942kg (13,100lb)
Dimensions: Length 12.11m (39ft 9in), Wingspan 17.14m (56ft 4in), Height 3m (9ft 10in)
Powerplant: Two 626kW (840hp) Bristol Mercury VIII nine-cylinder air-cooled engines
Maximum speed: 426km/h (265mph)

Range: 1481km (920 miles)
Ceiling: 7772m (25,500ft)
Crew: 2–3
Armament: Four 7.7mm (0.303in) machine guns in ventral pack and one 7.7mm (0.303in) Vickers K gun flexibly mounted in dorsal turret

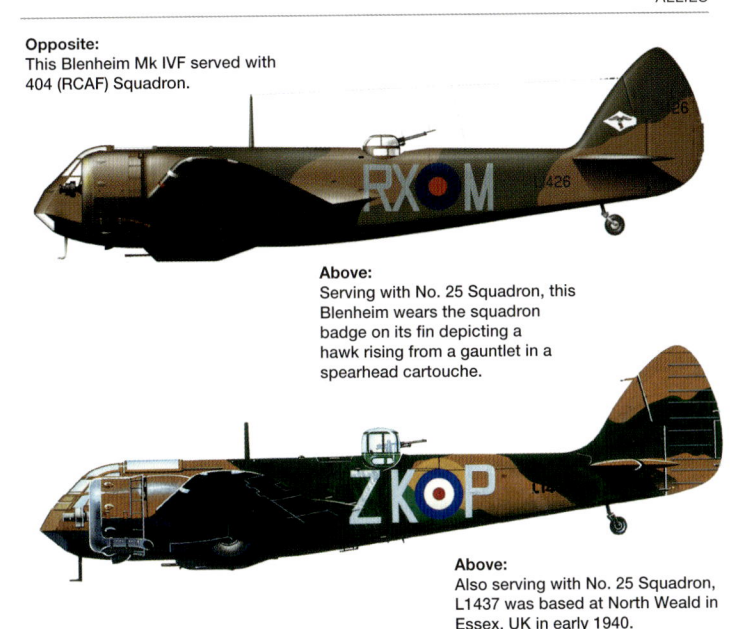

Opposite:
This Blenheim Mk IVF served with 404 (RCAF) Squadron.

Above:
Serving with No. 25 Squadron, this Blenheim wears the squadron badge on its fin depicting a hawk rising from a gauntlet in a spearhead cartouche.

Above:
Also serving with No. 25 Squadron, L1437 was based at North Weald in Essex, UK in early 1940.

war the Blenheim fighter operated by day, often used in concert with Blenheim bombers to strafe ground targets, but it was no match for the Bf 109 and was in the process of switching to night fighting during 1940. At the same time radar technology had advanced to the stage that it was possible to fit a radar set into an aircraft, and the Blenheim was of sufficient size to carry the bulky equipment.

Radar-guided night fighters
On the night of 23 July 1940, a radar-equipped Blenheim IF detected a Dornier Do 17 and then closed to shoot it down in the world's first airborne radar-guided interception. Subsequently six squadrons would fly night-fighter Blenheims, though the aircraft was rapidly replaced by the much more powerful Beaufighter. Blenheim Mk IVs used the same ventral gun pack, operating with some success, particularly in the Middle East and Mediterranean until mid 1941. Coastal Command also used the Blenheim IVF in conjunction with bomber Blenheims in the anti-shipping role.

Boulton Paul Defiant

A fighter with all of its armament concentrated in a turret and therefore able to attack from below or abeam, the Defiant was the only example of this concept to see RAF service.

The Defiant, which made its first flight on 11 August 1937, had been intended specifically as a destroyer of unescorted bombers, and with its second crewman and hydraulically operated turret, possessed a power-to-weight ratio some 25% worse than the Hurricane. As a result, performance, as expected, was not as good as either the Hurricane or the Spitfire but was still very respectable.

A gaggle of Defiants of No. 264 Squadron in flight during August 1940.

Boulton Paul Defiant Mk I

Weight: 3901kg (8600lb)
Dimensions: Length 10.77m (35ft 4in), Wingspan 11.99m (39ft 4in), Height 3.45m (11ft 4in)
Powerplant: One 770kW (1030hp) Rolls-Royce Merlin III V-12 liquid-cooled piston engine

Maximum speed: 489km/h (304mph)
Range: 748km (465 miles)
Ceiling: 9400m (31,000ft)
Crew: 2
Armament: Four 7.7mm (0.303in) Browning machine guns in dorsal turret

Opposite:
This Defiant was flown by Squadron Leader Philip Hunter, commander of 264 Squadron, and his gunner Pilot Officer Frederick King.

Above:
The ASR Mk I was equipped with an inflatable dinghy under each wing to be dropped to survivors in the water; this one flew with 277 Squadron.

Above:
This Defiant Mk II of 125 Squadron is finished in the overall matt black scheme adopted for night fighters.

At first, the aircraft did well, for example one squadron claimed 37 aircraft shot down without loss in a single day, but operations during the Battle of Britain were disastrous as the Defiant simply could not deal with the Bf 109.

Night fighter

Defiant units instead started to operate as night fighters from September 1940, claiming their first kills by the middle of the month. Radar was fitted to the Defiant during 1941 and it was briefly the most successful RAF night fighter before more powerful aircraft such as the Beaufighter appeared in numbers and the Defiant was withdrawn from combat during 1942. Defiants later served into 1943 as electronic-warfare aircraft initially carrying 'Moonshine' equipment that simulated large formations of aircraft and later with 'Mandrel', a noise jammer which overwhelmed enemy radar signals. The aircraft also performed the unglamorous but vital role of high-speed target tug until the end of the war.

de Havilland Mosquito

Designed as a bomber, the exceptional performance of the Mosquito saw a fighter version rapidly produced, becoming arguably the finest night fighter of the war.

Constructed largely of wood, the Mosquito used a minimum of strategic materials but was one of the fastest production aircraft in the world. Famously rejecting any sort of defensive gun armament in the name of greater performance, the aircraft was, however, designed with provision for *offensive* weapons. Fighter variants were fitted with four Hispano cannon as well as four machine guns, all

The NF Mk XIII was one of the night-fighter versions of the type, introduced in 1942.

de Havilland Mosquito NF Mk II

Weight: 9080kg (20,000lb)
Dimensions: Length 12.34m (40ft 6in), Wingspan 16.51m (54ft 2in), Height 4.66m (15ft 4in)
Powerplant: Two 1089kW (1480hp) Rolls-Royce Merlin 21 V-12 liquid-cooled piston engines
Maximum speed: 595km/h (370mph)

Range (internal fuel only): 1432km (890 miles)
Ceiling: 10,520m (34,500ft)
Crew: 2
Armament: Four 20mm (0.79in) Hispano cannon fixed, firing forward in lower forward fuselage and four 7.7mm (0.303in) Browning machine guns fixed, firing forward in nose

Opposite:
No. 157 Squadron was formed specifically to become the first Mosquito night fighter unit, taking the brand new Mosquito NF Mk II into operational service during April 1942.

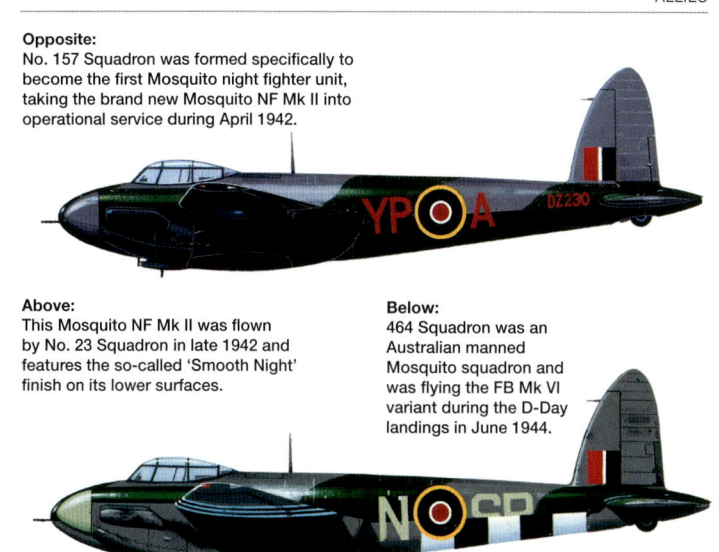

Above:
This Mosquito NF Mk II was flown by No. 23 Squadron in late 1942 and features the so-called 'Smooth Night' finish on its lower surfaces.

Below:
464 Squadron was an Australian manned Mosquito squadron and was flying the FB Mk VI variant during the D-Day landings in June 1944.

mounted in the fuselage. The cannon precluded the use of the ventral crew hatch of the bomber Mosquito, so a side door was fitted instead and the V-shaped windscreen was replaced by a single flat pane for better visibility, especially at night. A radar-equipped Mosquito night fighter achieved the type's first 'kill' in June 1942 and the Mosquito would serve as the principal British night fighter until the end of the war.

Fighter-bomber role
The aircraft also proved spectacularly successful in the fighter-bomber role, gaining fame for a succession of incredible pinpoint attacks on difficult targets utilizing the FB MK VI variant, such as Operation Jericho which breached the walls of Amiens jail. Later in the war the Mosquito was used to intercept V-1 flying bombs by night, destroying 623 of the missiles, and many were utilized to great effect by Coastal Command in anti-shipping strikes. The finest multirole aircraft of the war, Mosquitos were also built in both Canada and Australia and served for several years postwar.

Fairey Firefly

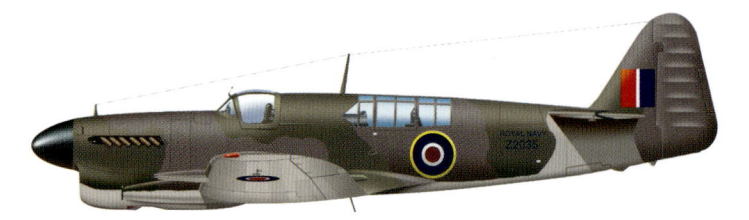

> **The Firefly superficially resembled the Fulmar which it replaced but it was a far more powerful and useful aircraft, remaining in frontline service into the Cold War era.**

The first Firefly, powered by the new Rolls-Royce Griffon engine, made its maiden flight on 22 December 1941. Flight testing was remarkably trouble free, the aircraft proving agile enough to out-turn the F6F Hellcat in tests in the US – although the Firefly was admitted to be slow, primarily due to the weight penalty imposed by the second crew member and associated equipment. The Firefly's first major

This is the seventh Firefly to come off the production line and is finished with the yellow undersides used on trials aircraft.

Fairey Firefly Mk I

Weight: 6375kg (14,054lb)
Dimensions: Length 11.45m (37ft 7in), Wingspan 13.56m (44ft 6in), Height 4.15m (13ft 7in)
Powerplant: One 970kW (1735hp) Rolls-Royce Griffon IIB V-12 liquid-cooled piston engine
Maximum speed: 509km/h (316mph)

Range: 2100km (1305 miles)
Ceiling: 8535m (28,000ft)
Crew: 2
Armament: Four 20mm (0.79in) Hispano cannon fixed firing forward in wings; up to 907kg (2000lb) bombload or eight 27kg (60lb) rockets under wings

Below:
The Firefly enjoyed a long and successful postwar career. This radar-equipped AS.5 was developed for the anti-submarine warfare role.

Opposite top:
Early Fireflies were fitted with a low profile canopy but headroom was so restricted that a considerably taller canopy was swiftly introduced, also conferring better visibility over the nose.

Right: A Firefly Mk I of No. 1770 Squadron, the first unit to take the type into action, is shown with its large Youngman flaps deployed, landing after a sortie in the Pacific theatre.

combat took place on 17 July 1944 when Fireflies took part in Operation Mascot, an attack on the German battleship Tirpitz in Norway.

Pacific service

However, most of the Firefly's wartime service took place with the British Pacific Fleet beginning with a series of strikes against oil refineries on Sumatra in January 1945. During these operations the Firefly scored its first aerial victories, shooting down two Nakajima Ki-43s. By July the Firefly was being used on strikes against the Japanese Home Islands and the aircraft became the first British type to fly over Tokyo. After the war the Firefly was developed into an anti-submarine warfare aircraft and saw action again during the Korean War. The last combat usage was in 1962 when Royal Netherlands Navy Fireflies conducted strikes against Indonesian forces in New Guinea.

Fairey Fulmar

Despite possessing a somewhat ponderous performance as a result of its two-seat configuration, the Fulmar shot down more enemy aircraft than any other British naval fighter.

The realization that the Blackburn Skua lacked the necessary speed to intercept several German bombers, such as the Ju 88, led the Air Ministry to issue a specification for a two-seat fighter/reconnaissance aircraft conforming to the contemporary view that a second crew member was essential for navigation at sea. Fairey adapted a pre-existing prototype, the P.4/34 light bomber, for carrier use to

An 807 Squadron Fulmar begins its take-off run as a second Fulmar and the Skuas of 800 Squadron warm up aboard HMS *Ark Royal* in 1941.

Fairey Fulmar Mk I

Weight: 4853kg (10,700lb)
Dimensions: Length 12.24m (40ft 2in), Wingspan 13.82m (46ft 4in), Height 3.25m (10ft 8in)
Powerplant: One 805kW (1080hp) Rolls-Royce Merlin VIII V-12 liquid-cooled piston engine

Maximum speed: 426km/h (265mph)
Range: 1287km (800 miles)
Ceiling: 6553m (21,500ft)
Crew: 2
Armament: Eight 7.7mm (0.303in) Browning machine guns fixed firing forward in wings; up to 91kg (200lb) bombload

Opposite:
Serving with No. 808 Squadron in the spring of 1941, N1860 displays the distinctive slender profile of the type.

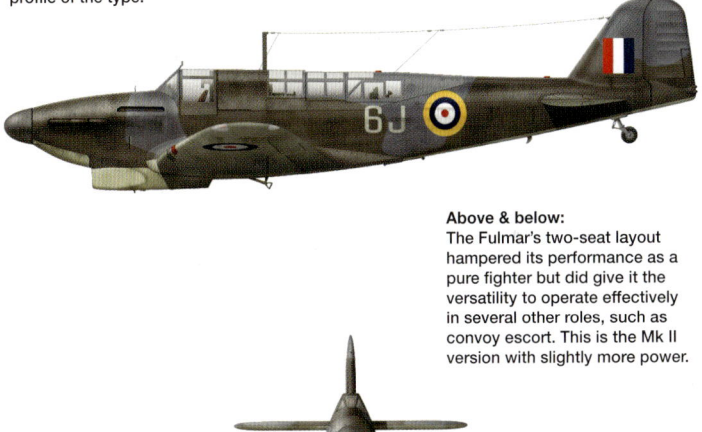

Above & below:
The Fulmar's two-seat layout hampered its performance as a pure fighter but did give it the versatility to operate effectively in several other roles, such as convoy escort. This is the Mk II version with slightly more power.

produce the Fulmar which flew on 4 January 1940 and although its performance was unspectacular, it was judged sufficient for an aircraft that was generally not expected to meet enemy single-seat fighters. Testing and clearance for service use was rapid, and within a year, seven squadrons were operating the type.

Cape Matapan

The Fulmar made its combat debut on 2 September 1940, when aircraft from HMS *Illustrious* shot down four Italian Savoia Marchetti SM.79 torpedo bombers and a Cant Z.501 flying boat in the Mediterranean. Fulmars subsequently provided top cover at the Battle of Cape Matapan, flew from escort carriers defending convoys in the Arctic Sea as well as in the Mediterranean and formed part of the fighter force during the Allied landings in North Africa. By 1943, the aircraft had generally been withdrawn from frontline use but a few remained operational as carrier night fighters until the end of the war.

Gloster Gladiator

The Gladiator saw widespread and intense action over the first two years or so of the war, fighting in Norway, France, Africa and the Mediterranean.

Designed by Henry Folland as a stopgap until the new eight-gun monoplane fighters appeared, the Gladiator first flew in September 1934 and curiously represented both the old and new, being the last British biplane fighter and simultaneously the first with an enclosed cockpit. Seven hundred and forty-seven were built until August 1939 and as newer fighters replaced the aircraft at home,

Differing from production aircraft in having an open cockpit, K5200 was the prototype Gladiator, flown here by test pilot Philip Sayer.

Gloster Gladiator Mk II

Weight: 2084kg (4594lb)
Dimensions: Length 8.36m (27ft 5in), Wingspan 9.83m (32ft 3in), Height 3.58m (10ft 7in)
Powerplant: One 620kW (830hp) Bristol Mercury IX 9-cylinder air-cooled radial piston engine

Maximum speed: 413km/h (257mph)
Range: 714km (444 miles)
Ceiling: 10,210m (33,500ft)
Crew: 1
Armament: Four 7.7mm (0.303in) Browning Mk II machine guns, two synchronized guns in fuselage sides and one fixed beneath each lower wing

Below (both images):
This Gladiator Mk I wears the colourful prewar markings of No. 79 Squadron RAF, based at Biggin Hill near London in 1937.

Opposite top:
N5520 is the only surviving Sea Gladiator of Malta's Hal Far Flight.

the Gladiator would perform most of its wartime service overseas. Although outclassed by modern fighters, the Gladiator's manoeuvrability could pose difficulties if it was well handled and it repeatedly scored victories against more advanced types, such as Bf 110s in Norway and the D.520 in Syria. The Gladiator's main foe for much of its career, however, was the Fiat CR.42 biplane, and the two were very closely matched in performance.

Naval variant

The Gladiator also served as a navalized variant for carrier use, the Sea Gladiator, with an arrester hook, naval radio and a dinghy pack carried between the undercarriage legs. Sea Gladiators performed the type's most famous action of all when for a time they formed the entire fighter defence of Malta, with never more than four airworthy at the same time, until the first Hurricanes arrived in early July 1940. The Gladiator performed well on the export market with ten nations all flying the type in addition to the UK, many of which saw action. The last Gladiator victory of all was attained by a Finnish example on 15 February 1943.

Gloster Meteor

> The Meteor, Britain's first operational jet combat aircraft, was a less radical design than the German Me 262 but proved an excellent basis for future development.

Gloster had built the E.28/39 research aircraft, the first British jet aircraft to fly, and George Carter, chief designer at Gloster was working on the design of a single-seat jet fighter even as the E.28/39 made its first flight. Two jet engines were considered necessary due to the low thrust of the early engines and apart from its groundbreaking powerplant the rest of the aircraft was fairly conventional,

At the end of World War II, Meteor development was proceeding rapidly and the Mk IV, pictured here, was in testing.

Gloster Meteor F Mk III

Weight: 6559kg (14,460lb)
Dimensions: Length 12.57m (41ft 3in), Wingspan 13.11m (43ft), Height 3.96 m (13ft)
Powerplant: Two Rolls-Royce Derwent I centrifugal flow turbojet engines, each rated at 8.9kN (2000lb) thrust

Maximum speed: 837km/h (515mph)
Range: 2160km (1350 miles)
Ceiling: 13,400m (43,950ft)
Crew: 1
Armament: Four 20mm (0.79in) hispano cannon fixed, firing forward in nose

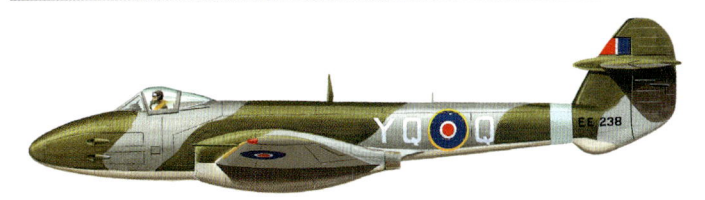

Opposite:
The fourth prototype, DG205/G was powered by Rover W2B engines. The 'G' suffix to the serial number denoted that the aircraft had to be under armed guard at all times.

Above & right:
EE238 was a Meteor Mk III that flew with 616 Squadron, the first RAF jet unit. This aircraft was destroyed in a fatal accident at an air display in May 1945; postwar RAF Meteor losses were truly appalling, with 890 lost in British service.

though it did feature a tricycle undercarriage for the first time on a British fighter. Three hundred production machines were ordered but nearly two years passed before the aircraft even flew due to slow engine development. Eventually the Meteor took to the air on 5 March 1943. By July 1944 the first production aircraft were being delivered to the RAF and the Meteor was quickly assigned to V-1 interception duties, its high speed at low altitude rendering it highly suitable for the task.

Meteor Mk III

Early 1945 saw two Meteor units operating on continental Europe though enemy air activity had dwindled to low levels and the Meteors were used on ground attack duties. By the end of the war the first examples of the much-improved Meteor Mk III had entered service and postwar the aircraft was developed into a wide variety of variants, eventually becoming the most produced British jet aircraft with 3947 built.

Hawker Hurricane

Victor of the Battle of Britain, the Hurricane was the most important British fighter during the first two years of the war. It was built in vast numbers and widely exported.

The Hurricane was the first British combat aircraft capable of exceeding 483km/h (300mph) as well as being the Royal Air Force's first 'modern' monoplane fighter with retractable undercarriage. Developed as a monoplane version of the Hawker Fury biplane, the Hurricane flew for the first time on 6 November 1935. Hawker began preparations for mass production even before an order had

The final production variant, the Mk IV, could be fitted with a variety of weaponry, including two underwing 40mm (1.57in) cannon. In this guise it was designated the Mk IVD.

Hawker Hurricane Mk I

Weight: 3024kg (6661lb)
Dimensions: Length 9.58m (31ft 5in), Wingspan 12.19m (40ft), Height 3.95m (12ft 11.5in)
Powerplant: One 770kW (1030hp) Rolls-Royce Merlin III V-12 liquid-cooled piston engine

Maximum speed: 508km/h (316mph)
Range: 445km (716 miles)
Ceiling: 10,120m (33,200ft)
Crew: 1
Armament: Eight 7.7mm (0.303in) Browning machine guns fixed, firing forward in wings

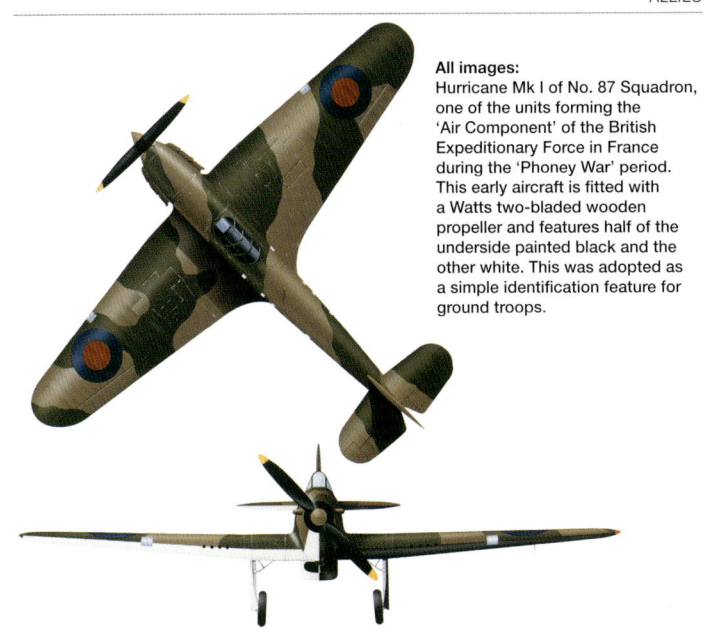

All images:
Hurricane Mk I of No. 87 Squadron, one of the units forming the 'Air Component' of the British Expeditionary Force in France during the 'Phoney War' period. This early aircraft is fitted with a Watts two-bladed wooden propeller and features half of the underside painted black and the other white. This was adopted as a simple identification feature for ground troops.

been placed and thus significant numbers of Hurricanes were available by the outbreak of war. By 1940, the majority of British fighters were Hurricanes and they famously destroyed more enemy aircraft than all other defences combined during the Battle of Britain. This action also demonstrated that the Spitfire was the better air superiority interceptor and consequently the Hurricane would be utilized in a greater variety of roles and sent overseas in large numbers earlier than the Supermarine fighter.

Hurricane Mk II
During 1940 the Hurricane Mk II appeared and this would be built in the greatest numbers, most being armed with four cannon as the Mk IIC, though a tank-buster variant, the Mk IID, with 40mm (1.57in) cannon was also produced. The Hurricane was increasingly used as a ground attack aircraft from 1941, this gradually becoming its most important role, and it was utilized as a close support asset until the end of the war.

Hawker Sea Hurricane

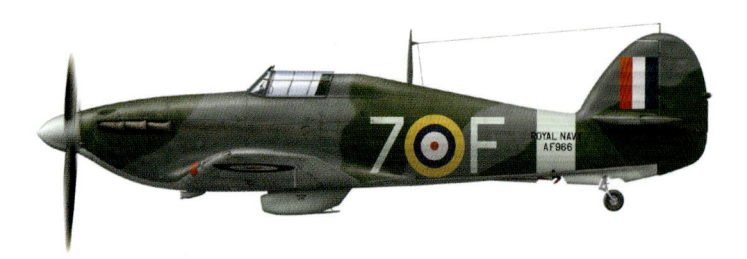

The versatile Hurricane became an important asset for the Fleet Air Arm, providing the Navy with a better fighter than the Fulmar at its moment of greatest need.

Initial Hurricane use at sea saw the aircraft employed in a semi-disposable fashion aboard CAM (catapult armed merchantman) ships specifically to combat the Focke Wulf Condor. When a Condor was sighted, the Hurricane was fired from a crude rocket catapult to either shoot down or chase away the enemy aircraft. The pilot could then bail out, fly to land if within range, or ditch. The

The four 20mm (0.78in) cannons are prominent on this Sea Hurricane Mk IIC.

Hawker Sea Hurricane Mk IIC

Weight: 3511kg (7740lb)
Dimensions: Length 9.83m (32ft 4in), Wingspan 12.2m (40ft), Height 4m (13ft 1in)
Powerplant: One 954kW (1280hp) Rolls-Royce Merlin XX V-12 liquid-cooled piston engine

Maximum speed: 505km/h (314mph)
Range: 1207km (750 miles)
Ceiling: 10,516m (34,500ft)
Crew: 1
Armament: Four 20mm (0.78in) Hispano cannon fixed firing forward in wings

Above:
This Sea Hurricane was flying with No. 835 Squadron in June 1944. This unit adopted an all-over white scheme to conceal the aircraft against the prevailing overcast of the North Atlantic.

Opposite top:
Z7015 served with No. 880 Squadron during 1941. This airframe was built in Canada as a standard Hurricane and was modified for naval use in the UK.

Above:
No. 800 Squadron Sea Hurricane XII during the Operation Torch landings of November 1942. American markings were universally applied during Torch.

Sea Hurricane subsequently appeared in navalized form with an arrester hook and strengthened structure for carrier landings. Entering service in July 1941, the carrier-capable Sea Hurricane scored its first victory on the last day of that month when a Dornier Do 18 was shot down.

Over the following two years the Sea Hurricane saw considerable action, notably during Operation Pedestal of August 1942, when a convoy of 14 fast merchant ships fought their way through near constant attacks to Malta with desperately needed supplies. The Hurricane was never entirely adapted for carrier use, folding wings never being produced for it, and only two carriers, HMS *Eagle* and HMS *Ark Royal,* had deck lifts big enough to accommodate the Hurricane. Both had been lost by August 1942 and as a result Sea Hurricanes had to be stored, exposed to the elements, on the deck of the Navy's remaining carriers, limiting the amount that could be carried to approximately six aircraft each.

Hawker Typhoon

Initially plagued with engine, structural and aerodynamic issues, the Typhoon endured a problematic introduction to service to become one of the most potent close-support aircraft of the war.

Initially designed as a Hurricane replacement, the Typhoon was not an unqualified success as an air superiority fighter. Aerodynamic problems due to its thick wings meant its performance was not as good as predicted and a quirk of the tail's design resulted in the rear fuselage sometimes failing in flight. The latter turned out to be a simple problem to cure but the cause was difficult to

An early Hawker Typhoon Mk IB, with the heavily framed 'car door' style cockpit, carrying eight rocket projectiles.

Hawker Typhoon Mk IB

Weight: 6010kg (13,250lb)
Dimensions: Length 9.74m (31ft 11.5in), Wingspan 12.67m (41ft 7in), Height 4.67m (15ft 4in)
Powerplant: One 1630kW (2180hp) Napier Sabre IIA H-24 liquid-cooled piston engine
Maximum speed: 679km/h (422mph)

Range (internal fuel only): 1110km (690 miles)
Ceiling: 9700m (31,800ft)
Crew: 1
Armament: Four 20mm (0.79in) Hispano cannon fixed, forward firing in wings; up to 908kg (2000lb) bombload or eight rockets under wings

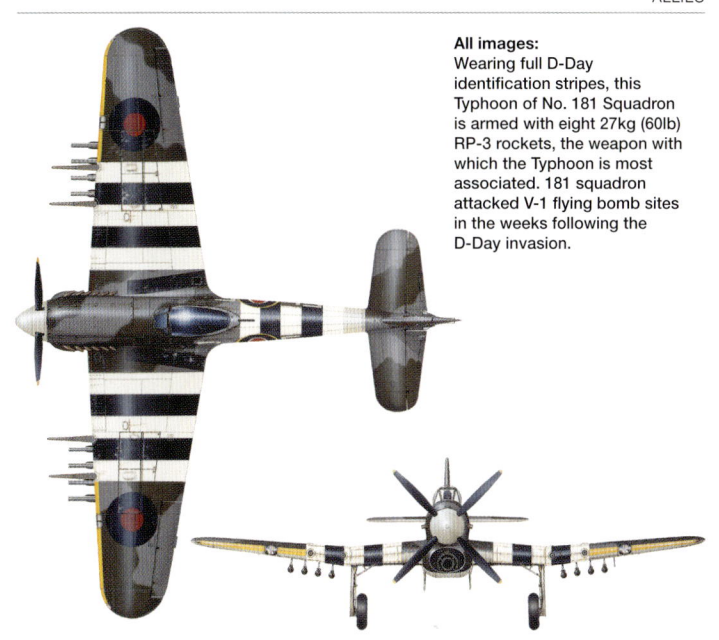

All images:
Wearing full D-Day identification stripes, this Typhoon of No. 181 Squadron is armed with eight 27kg (60lb) RP-3 rockets, the weapon with which the Typhoon is most associated. 181 squadron attacked V-1 flying bomb sites in the weeks following the D-Day invasion.

ascertain and led to several fatal accidents before it was fixed. The Napier Sabre engine also initially gave trouble; it was at an early state of development when committed to service and regularly failed but reliability had improved massively by the end of the war. The Typhoon had flown for the first time on 24 February 1940, entering service in September 1941 as the Royal Air Force's first combat aircraft able to exceed 644km/h (400mph) in level flight.

Powerful fighter-bomber
Despite the initial problems the Typhoon became invaluable as the only aircraft capable of intercepting the low altitude 'tip and run' bombing attacks on coastal targets being made by Fw 190s. Subsequently the addition of underwing bomb racks, followed by the fitting of rails for four 27kg (60lb) RP-3 rockets under each wing, transformed the aircraft into a powerful and effective fighter-bomber utilized for devastating close support attacks in the breakout from Normandy until the end of the war in Europe.

Hawker Tempest

Possibly Britain's finest single-seat piston-engined fighter, the Tempest was developed as a variant of the Typhoon, intended to cure the worst of its aerodynamic foibles.

Designer Sydney Camm and his team redesigned the Typhoon's wing, reducing its thickness overall. This left insufficient room inside the wing for fuel tanks, meaning the fuselage had to be lengthened to accommodate fuel which in turn required larger tail surfaces. The changes were such that the aircraft was considered a new type and the name Tempest was bestowed on the aircraft which made its first flight on 2 September 1942.

Tempests of 501 Squadron; Squadron Leader Joe Berry assumed command of 501 in August 1944 and became the top-scoring anti V-1 pilot with 59 destroyed.

Hawker Tempest Mk V

Weight: 6340kg (13,977lb)
Dimensions: Length 10.26m (33ft 8in), Wingspan 12.5m (41ft), Height 4.52m (14ft 10in)
Powerplant: One 1800kW (2420hp) Napier Sabre IIB H-24 liquid-cooled piston engine
Maximum speed: 700km/h (435mph)

Range (internal fuel only): 680km (420 miles)
Ceiling: 11,100m (36,500ft)
Crew: 1
Armament: Four 20mm (0.79in) Hispano cannon fixed, forward firing in wings; up to 908kg (2000lb) bombload

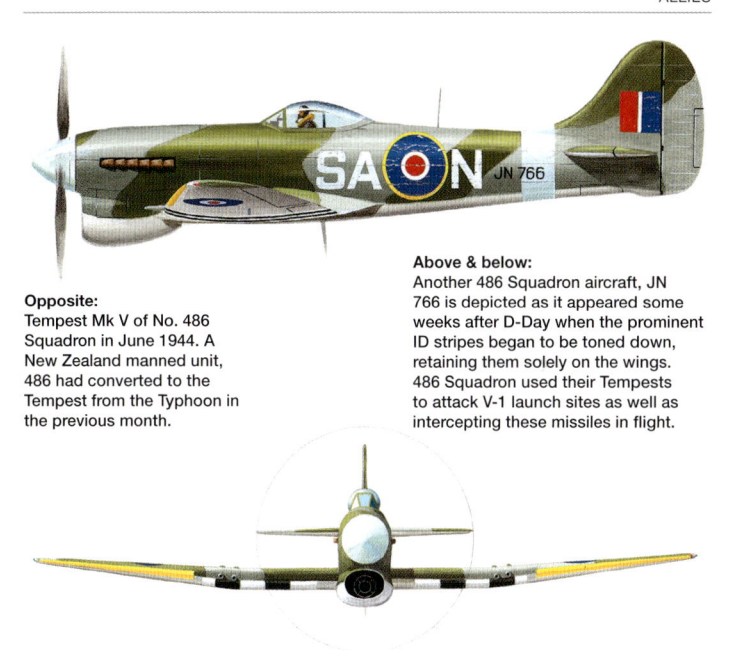

Opposite:
Tempest Mk V of No. 486 Squadron in June 1944. A New Zealand manned unit, 486 had converted to the Tempest from the Typhoon in the previous month.

Above & below:
Another 486 Squadron aircraft, JN 766 is depicted as it appeared some weeks after D-Day when the prominent ID stripes began to be toned down, retaining them solely on the wings. 486 Squadron used their Tempests to attack V-1 launch sites as well as intercepting these missiles in flight.

Flight testing revealed that the new wing markedly improved handling and performance and the aircraft entered service in April 1944. During June the Tempest scored its first victories, claiming four Bf 109s destroyed over the Normandy beachhead before switching to defence against the V-1 guided missile.

Doodlebug destroyer

With its excellent speed at low altitude, the Tempest proved particularly effective in this role and accounted for 638 V-1s destroyed between June and August 1944, the most of any aircraft type. Subsequently the Tempest followed the Allied armies across Europe, acting primarily as an air superiority fighter at medium and low level but also undertaking ground attack duties. By the end of the war the Tempest II was in production powered by the Bristol Centaurus radial, and the Tempest would serve the postwar RAF until 1950.

Supermarine Spitfire Mks I–V
(early Merlin variants)

Built in larger numbers than any other British aircraft, the iconic Spitfire remained in production and frontline service throughout World War II.

Supermarine's Type 300, later named Spitfire, made its maiden flight on 6 March 1936 and underwent RAF trials in July, demonstrating outstanding performance and resulting in glowing praise from test pilots, but initial production was delayed and the first production aircraft entered service only in August 1938. Spitfires were deliberately held back from the fighting in France before being

Spitfire Mk Is of No. 19 Squadron, the first unit to fly the Spitfire, photographed at Duxford airfield, Cambridgeshire, in 1939.

Supermarine Spitfire Mk I

Weight: 2651kg (5844lb)
Dimensions: Length 9.12m (29ft 11in), Wingspan 11.23m (36ft 10in), Height 3.86m (9ft 10in)
Powerplant: One 770kW (1030hp) Rolls-Royce Merlin II or III V-12 liquid-cooled piston engine

Maximum speed: 557km/h (346mph)
Range: 1014km (630 miles)
Ceiling: 9296m (30,500ft)
Crew: 1
Armament: Eight 7.7mm (0.303in) Browning machine guns fixed, firing forward in wings

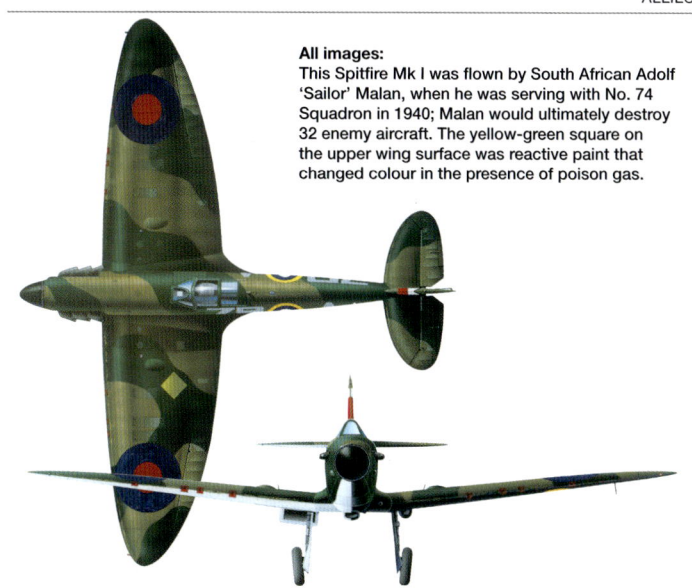

All images:
This Spitfire Mk I was flown by South African Adolf 'Sailor' Malan, when he was serving with No. 74 Squadron in 1940; Malan would ultimately destroy 32 enemy aircraft. The yellow-green square on the upper wing surface was reactive paint that changed colour in the presence of poison gas.

committed to the subsequent Battle of Britain which led to the Spitfire attaining a level of popular fame never exceeded by a British military aircraft before or since. During the battle, Spitfires scored more kills relative to the total fleet size than Hurricanes and would effectively become the primary British air superiority asset for the rest of the war. Remarkably well matched with its primary opponent, the Bf 109E, in overall performance the early Spitfire was somewhat more manoeuvrable but less well armed with its rifle-calibre machine guns.

Mk V

The Spitfire Mks I and II differed only in the variant of Merlin engine fitted but the majority of the subsequent fighter variant, the Mk V, featured an armament of two 20mm (0.79in) cannon and four machine guns as well as a more powerful Merlin 45 engine. The Mk V was built in larger numbers than any other Spitfire variant and was the first to serve overseas, in Malta, with examples subsequently operating elsewhere in the Mediterranean, as well as North Africa, USSR and the South West Pacific. The aircraft also operated highly successfully as a long-range reconnaissance machine.

Supermarine Spitfire Mks VII–XVI
(late Merlin variants)

Later Merlin-powered Spitfire development was driven by the appearance of the Fw 190, superior to the Mk V Spitfire in every performance parameter except turn rate.

When the Fw 190 appeared, Supermarine had been working in parallel on the improved Mk VII, intended for the high-altitude role and featuring a pressurized cockpit, and the medium-altitude Mk VIII. Neither aircraft was expected to be ready for several months and the extemporized Mk IX resulted from a trial fitting of the Merlin 61 engine into a standard Mk V airframe. The result was dramatic, with

No. 611 'West Lancashire' Squadron, based at Biggin Hill, was one of the first units to convert to the Spitfire Mk IX in July 1942.

Supermarine Spitfire F Mk IX

Weight: 4309kg (9500lb)
Dimensions: Length 9.47m (31ft 1in), Wingspan 11.23m (36ft 10in), Height 3.86m (12ft 8in)
Powerplant: One 1151kw (1565hp) Rolls-Royce Merlin 61 liquid cooled V-12 piston engine
Maximum speed: 657km/h (408mph)

Range: 698km (434 miles)
Ceiling: 13,106m (43,000ft)
Crew: 1
Armament: Two 20mm (0.79in) Hispano cannon and four 7.7mm (0.303in) Browning machine guns, or four 20mm (0.79in) Hispano cannon in wings; up to 460kg (1000lb) bombload

All images:
One of the first Mk IXs to be completed, BS459 flew with No. 306 'Torun' Squadron, a Polish-manned unit based at Northolt, West London, UK. This unit was engaged in fighter sweeps over occupied France during early 1943.

top speed increased by around 113km/h (70mph) and fighting altitude improved by around 3000m (10,000ft). The first Mk IXs entered operational service in mid 1942, immediately demonstrating a marked superiority over the Fw 190, and would remain in frontline service until the end of the war.

Overseas service

The Mk VII was eventually built only in trivial numbers and the VIII, though it was mass produced, was outnumbered by the somewhat improvised Mk IX, and the vast majority of those built would serve overseas, including significant numbers supplied to the USAAF in North Africa and Italy. Later examples of the Mk IX, Mk VIII and Mk XVI (identical to the IX but fitted with an American-built Packard Merlin) were increasingly used as ground attack aircraft as the war progressed and Axis air activity lessened.

Supermarine Spitfire Mks XII –Mk 21 (Griffon variants)

By 1944 the emphasis of Spitfire development had switched to a completely new version with a larger capacity and a significantly more powerful engine: the Rolls-Royce Griffon.

Originally developed for naval use, the Griffon was of 10 litres (2.64 gallons) greater capacity than the Merlin and optimized for low-level use. Although promising, its development had been delayed by the urgent need for Merlins but the Griffon-powered Mk IV eventually made its first flight in late 1941. However, the appearance of Fw 190 'tip and run' raiders capable of outrunning Mk IX Spitfires at low level

Mk XIVs of No. 610 'County of Chester' Squadron in 1944.

Supermarine Spitfire FR Mk XIVE

Weight: 3856kg (8500lb)
Dimensions: Length 9.96m (32ft 8in), Wingspan 11.23m (36ft 10in), Height 3.86m (12ft 8in)
Powerplant: One 1529kW (2050hp) Rolls-Royce Griffon 65 liquid cooled V-12 piston engine
Maximum speed: 721km/h (448mph)

Range (internal fuel only): 740km (460 miles)
Ceiling: 13,564m (44,500ft)
Crew: 1
Armament: Two 20mm (0.79in) Hispano cannon and four 7.7mm (0.303in) Browning machine guns, or four 20mm Hispano cannon in wings; up to 460kg (1000lb) bombload

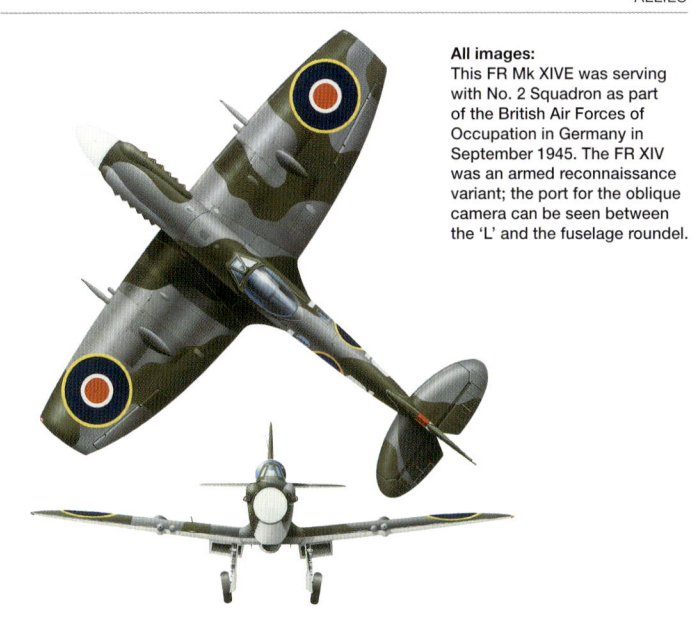

All images:
This FR Mk XIVE was serving with No. 2 Squadron as part of the British Air Forces of Occupation in Germany in September 1945. The FR XIV was an armed reconnaissance variant; the port for the oblique camera can be seen between the 'L' and the fuselage roundel.

saw the rapid introduction of the Mk XII, essentially a Mk IX airframe fitted with a Griffon engine, which entered service in mid 1942. Although only 100 were built, they were worked hard, ending their service lives intercepting V-1 flying bombs in the summer of 1944.

Mk XIV

The more extensively modified Mk XIV, which would become the most produced Griffon variant, entered service in January 1944 after it had been found to have 'the best all-round performance of any present-day fighter' in tests. This assessment was confirmed in combat, though the rapid reduction in German aviation activity resulted in fewer encounters with enemy aircraft by the time the Mk XIV was in service. The final development was the Mk 21 with a new wing but only one squadron had equipped with this variant before the end of hostilities. As with the Merlin-powered aircraft, the Griffon Spitfire was developed as a successful photo-reconnaissance aircraft and it was in this form that the Spitfire made its last operational flight with the RAF in April 1954.

Supermarine Seafire

The Spitfire did not adapt easily to carrier operations but nonetheless saw widespread use, covering the Anzio landings in 1943 and serving with the British Pacific Fleet until VJ day.

Admiralty requests to develop a navalized Spitfire were rejected, mainly for financial reasons, until late 1941 when work on a carrier-capable Spitfire began in earnest. The name 'Sea Spitfire' was officially adopted but this was immediately shortened to 'Seafire', which subsequently became the official name of the aircraft. Early Seafires were minimal conversions of RAF Spitfires with A-frame arrester

Seafire development continued beyond VJ day. This is a Rolls-Royce Griffon-powered Seafire Mk XVII of 1833 Naval Air Squadron which flew this variant in 1947.

Supermarine Seafire F Mk III

Weight: 3280kg (7232lb)
Dimensions: Length 9.2m (30ft 3in), Wingspan 11.23m (36ft 10in), Height 3.49m (11ft 6in)
Powerplant: One 1182kW (1585hp) Rolls-Royce Merlin 55 V-12 liquid-cooled piston engine
Maximum speed: 578km/h (359mph)
Range: 748km (465 miles)

Ceiling: 11,000m (36,000ft)
Crew: 1
Armament: Two 20mm (0.79in) Hispano cannon and four 12.7mm (0.5in) Browning machine guns fixed firing forward in wings; up to 226kg (500lb) bombload or eight 27kg (60lb) rockets under wings

Above:
This Mk 47, the last Seafire variant, flew combat missions over Malaya and Korea with 800 NAS.

Opposite top:
MB270 was built in December 1942 but its career ended in October 1944 when it was written off following a barrier strike on HMS *Attacker* near Crete.

Above:
Sub Lieutenant Richard Reynolds of 894 Naval Air Squadron shot down down two Mitsubishi A6M Zeros in this aircraft on 31 March 1945.

hooks and naval equipment fitted, but the development of a folding wing system resulted in the Seafire Mk III, a much more useful carrier aircraft, with deliveries starting in April 1943. The Seafire inherited the Spitfire's excellent handling in the air, and in combat both in Europe and the Pacific it proved highly effective.

Poor deck landing

Unfortunately it also gained a reputation as a poor deck-landing aircraft, with a tendency to 'float' on landing resulting in it regularly failing to catch an arrester wire and winding up in the crash barrier. Even if an arrester wire was caught, the position of the hook under the fuselage resulted in a sharp nose-down pitch, sometimes causing the propeller to strike the deck, and the undercarriage was prone to collapse. Nevertheless the urgent requirement for naval fighters resulted in the worst of the aircraft's traits being ameliorated and the Seafire became the most produced British naval fighter of the war.

Westland Whirlwind

Highly advanced and formidable, the Whirlwind was the first cannon-armed fighter to enter RAF service but production was limited due to the cancellation of its engine.

Designer Teddy Petter's small twin-engine fighter possessed such radical features as the first clear-view perspex bubble canopy seen on a British aircraft, a monocoque fuselage, T-tail and ducted radiators fitted in the wing leading edge. Flying for the first time on 11 October 1938, the Whirlwind demonstrated excellent performance and when fitted with its armament of four Hispano 20mm (0.79in) cannon, it

Pictured during trials, this Whirlwind Mk I is carrying a 226kg (500lb) bomb under each wing.

Westland Whirlwind

Weight: 5191kg (11,445lb)
Dimensions: Length 9.83m (32ft 3in), Wingspan 13.72m (32ft 3in), Height 3.35m (11ft)
Powerplant: Two 660kW (885hp) Rolls-Royce Peregrine V-12 liquid-cooled piston engines
Maximum speed: 580km/h (360mph)

Range: 1300km (800 miles)
Ceiling: 9200m (30,300ft)
Crew: 1
Armament: Four 20mm (0.79in) Hispano cannon fixed firing forward in nose; up to 460kg (1000lb) bombload under wings

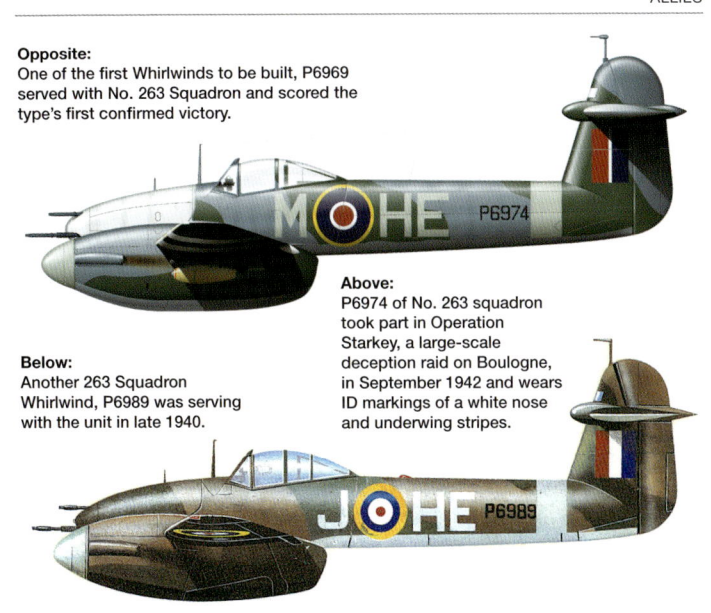

Opposite:
One of the first Whirlwinds to be built, P6969 served with No. 263 Squadron and scored the type's first confirmed victory.

Above:
P6974 of No. 263 squadron took part in Operation Starkey, a large-scale deception raid on Boulogne, in September 1942 and wears ID markings of a white nose and underwing stripes.

Below:
Another 263 Squadron Whirlwind, P6989 was serving with the unit in late 1940.

was, for a time, the most heavily armed fighter in the world. Unfortunately Rolls-Royce was compelled to stop production of the Peregrine engine, which was only used by the Whirlwind, to concentrate on the much more widely empoyed Merlin and with no alternative engine available only 114 Whirlwinds were built, equipping just two squadrons.

Convoy patrols

In service the aircraft proved highly effective. Operations began with convoy patrols and anti E-boat missions and the Whirlwind scored its first confirmed victory on 8 February 1941, shooting down an Arado Ar 196 floatplane. Underwing bomb racks were added during 1942 allowing the carriage of either two 227kg (500lb) or two 113kg (250lb) bombs. In this guise, unofficially named 'Whirlibombers', the aircraft engaged in ground attack duties against targets of opportunity in occupied Europe until the aircraft was replaced in November 1943 by the Typhoon, a remarkably long period of frontline operational service at this stage of the war.

Bell P-39 Airacobra

Although it proved disappointing in USAAF service, the P-39 achieved great success in the Soviet Union, proving more popular than any other lend-lease fighter.

An unusual design, the P-39 utilized an Oldsmobile 37mm (1.45in) firing straight through the propeller spinner with the engine mounted behind the cockpit, using an extension shaft to drive the propeller. The concentration of weight on the aircraft's centre of gravity conferred excellent manoeuvrability and the removal of the engine from the nose provided room for more guns and a

P-39Q on test in the US. This variant was produced specifically for Soviet use and the vast majority went to the Eastern Front.

Bell P-39N Airacobra

Weight: 3995kg (8800lb)
Dimensions: Length 9.21m (30ft 2in), Wingspan 10.37m (34ft), Height 3.6m (11ft 10in)
Powerplant: One 895kW (1200hp) Allison V-1710-85 V-12 liquid-cooled piston engine
Maximum speed: 605km/h (376mph)
Range (with drop tank): 1570km (975 miles)
Ceiling: 11,665m (38,270ft)

Crew: 1
Armament: One 37mm (1.46in) M4 Cannon fixed firing through propeller spinner; two 12.7mm (0.5in) Colt-Browning M2 machine guns fixed forward firing in fuselage nose; two 7.62mm (0.3in) Browning M1919 machine guns fixed forward firing in wings; up to 227kg (500lb) bombload under fuselage

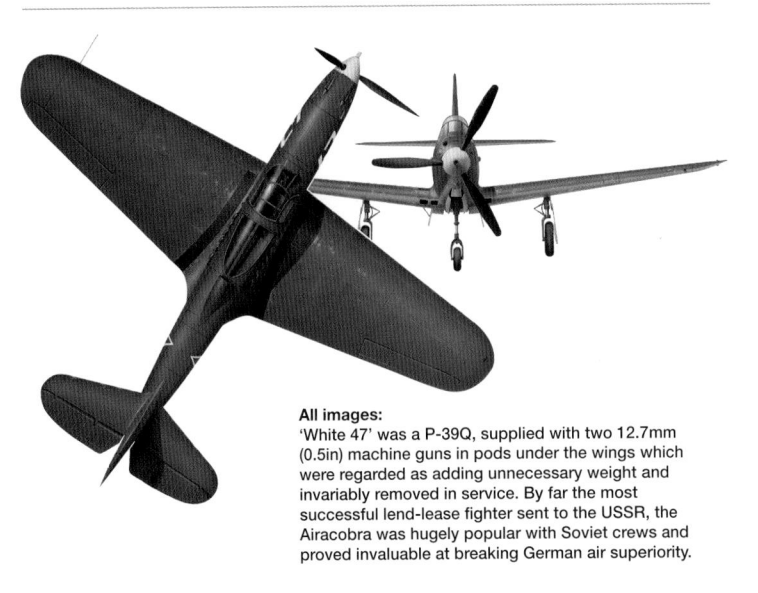

All images:
'White 47' was a P-39Q, supplied with two 12.7mm (0.5in) machine guns in pods under the wings which were regarded as adding unnecessary weight and invariably removed in service. By far the most successful lend-lease fighter sent to the USSR, the Airacobra was hugely popular with Soviet crews and proved invaluable at breaking German air superiority.

nosewheel undercarriage (another novel feature). Initially flown on 6 April 1938, the prototype featured a turbocharger and demonstrated excellent performance. Unfortunately, the turbocharger proved unreliable and the Air Corps weren't interested in high-altitude operations anyway so it was discarded, limiting the P-39 to medium- and low-level use. P-39s performed adequately if not spectacularly in the Pacific but were quickly sidelined in Western Europe and offloaded on the Soviets.

Eastern Front flier

However, Bell had accidentally designed an aircraft perfectly suited to conditions on the Eastern Front: it was well armed, fast at low altitude and manoeuvrable, and Soviet pilots rated it equal, or superior, to the Bf 109 and Fw 190. The P-39 was also tough, its tricycle landing gear well suited to rough fields, and many Soviet pilots claimed high scores with the *Kobrushka* ('little Cobra'). Most successful of all was Grigory Rechkalov who shot down 48 of his 54 confirmed 'kills' in the Bell fighter, the highest score achieved by any pilot worldwide in a US-built fighter.

Bell P-63 Kingcobra

Utilizing the same unconventional layout as the P-39, the Kingcobra was in fact a completely new design. The majority of P-63s built were supplied to the USSR.

Fitted with a new laminar flow wing, the Kingcobra featured the same armament of two 12.7mm (0.5in) Browning machine guns and one 37mm (1.5in) Oldsmobile cannon firing through the propeller spinner, augmented by two further machine guns in underwing fairings. Unlike the P-39, it featured a second supercharger specifically for high-altitude performance, which proved

This RP-63E manned target aircraft has survived in the collection of the USAF Museum. The US did not employ the Kingcobra in combat.

Bell P-63A

Weight: 4853kg (10,700lb)
Dimensions: Length 9.96m (32ft 8in), Wingspan 11.68m (38ft 4in), Height 3.84m (12ft 7in)
Powerplant: One 1,300kW (1,800hp) Allison V-1710-117 V-12 liquid-cooled piston engine
Speed: 660km/h (410mph)

Range: 720km (450 miles)
Ceiling: 13,000m (43,000ft)
Crew: 1
Armament: One 37mm (1.5in) M10 cannon, four 12.7mm (0.5in) Browning M2 machine guns; up to 680kg (1500lb) bombload

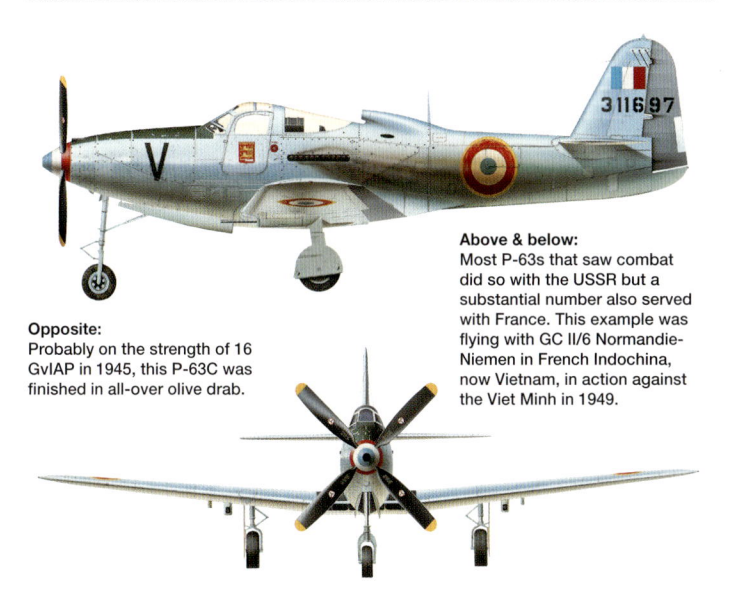

Above & below:
Most P-63s that saw combat did so with the USSR but a substantial number also served with France. This example was flying with GC II/6 Normandie-Niemen in French Indochina, now Vietnam, in action against the Viet Minh in 1949.

Opposite:
Probably on the strength of 16 GvIAP in 1945, this P-63C was finished in all-over olive drab.

effective. Although flown on 7 December 1942, deliveries only began in October 1943 by which time the P-51 was available, which the USAAF rated as superior, but development and production were authorized mainly for supply to Allied nations, primarily the Soviet Union, though France also received significant numbers of P-63s. Ultimately, 3303 Kingcobras would roll out of Bell's factory and of those 2421 were flown, via Canada, Alaska and across the Bering sea to the Soviet Union.

Soviet service

Officially, an agreement between the USSR and US restricted the Kingcobra to the Pacific area of operations, where the type attained its first confirmed victory on 15 August 1945 when Lieutenant I. F. Miroshnichenko destroyed a Ki-43 Hayabusa. There is considerable evidence that P-63s were, however, secretly used against Germany in the last days of the war in Europe. In the USSR the P-63 proved popular and was retained in frontline Soviet service until 1951, receiving the NATO reporting name 'Fred'.

Brewster F2 Buffalo

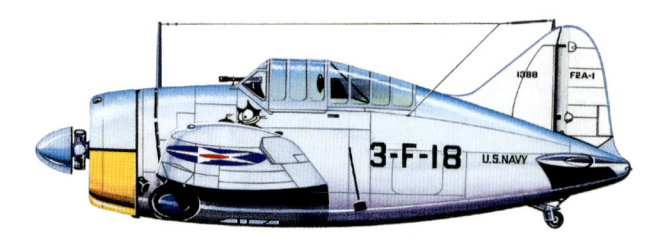

The US Navy's first monoplane fighter, the F2A proved disappointing when committed to combat against the Japanese but achieved greater success with other nations.

First flown on 2 December 1937, the XF2A-1 could not be described as sleek but it boasted a flush riveted stressed skin construction, split flaps and hydraulically powered retractable undercarriage. The first examples were aboard USS *Saratoga* by the end of 1939, becoming the first operational monoplane carrier fighters in the US Navy, and initial operations at sea proved relatively trouble free.

Although sidelined as a fighter in US service, the F2A proved to be an excellent advanced trainer because of its docile handling.

Brewster F2A-3

Weight: 3247kg (7159lb)
Dimensions: Length 8.03m (26ft 4in), Wingspan 10.67m (35ft), Height 3.66m (12ft)
Powerplant: One 890kW (1200hp) Wright R-1820-40 Cyclone 9-cylinder air-cooled engine
Speed: 517km/h (321mph)
Range: 1553km (965 miles)

Ceiling: 10,100m (33,200ft)
Crew: 1
Armament: Two 12.7mm (0.5in) M2 Browning machine guns fixed forward firing in wings, two 12.7mm (0.5in) M2 Browning machine guns fixed forward firing in cowling; up to two 90kg (200lb) bombs under wings

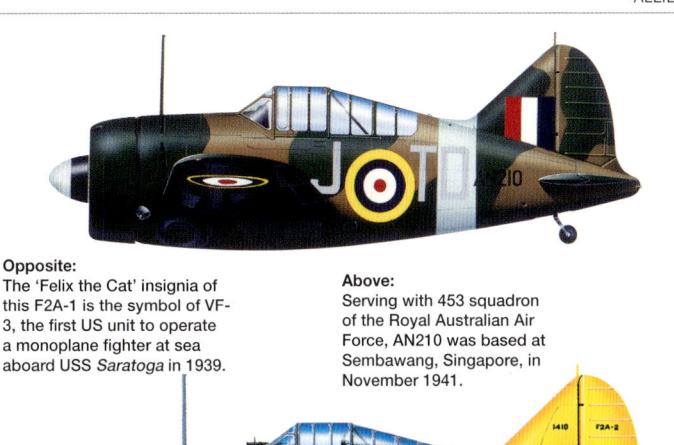

Opposite:
The 'Felix the Cat' insignia of this F2A-1 is the symbol of VF-3, the first US unit to operate a monoplane fighter at sea aboard USS *Saratoga* in 1939.

Above:
Serving with 453 squadron of the Royal Australian Air Force, AN210 was based at Sembawang, Singapore, in November 1941.

Above:
VF-2, the 'Flying Chiefs', took their F2A-2s aboard USS *Lexington* in March 1941.

At around the same time orders were received from Finland, Belgium and the United Kingdom, the latter nation naming the aircraft 'Buffalo' which later became a universal nickname for the aircraft.

The F2A's only major engagement in US service occurred during the Battle of Midway when poor tactics saw Marine Corps unit VMF-221 lose 13 out of 20 F2As committed. All US F2As were subsequently relegated to advanced training, a role for which their easy flying characteristics and relatively high performance made them eminently suitable. By contrast, in Finland, Brewsters proved both highly successful and popular with pilots, achieving a startling victory to loss ratio of 32 to one. In Britain, however, the Buffalo was rejected for use in Europe and most were sent to the Far East in the complacent belief they would be superior to any Japanese fighter. In reality, the Brewsters were outnumbered and outperformed by modern Japanese fighters and nearly all had been destroyed in fierce fighting by March 1942.

Curtiss P-36 and Hawk 75

The first US air-to-air victories of World War II were achieved by the P-36 but the aircraft would see most action in French and Finnish hands.

Although it lost the competition to select the first US monoplane fighter to the Seversky P-35, the P-36 possessed enough merit for development to continue. A change of engine greatly improved performance and the P-36 subsequently received the largest US military aircraft order since 1918. Meanwhile, Curtiss was busy marketing a simplified export version with fixed landing gear dubbed

This USAAC P-36C wears a temporary camouflage scheme for exercises in 1939.

Curtiss P-36A

Weight: 2726kg (6010lb)
Dimensions: Length 8.69m (28ft 6in), Wingspan 11.38m (37ft 4in), Height 2.57m (8ft 5in)
Powerplant: One 780kW 1050(hp) Pratt & Whitney R-1830-17 Twin Wasp 14-cylinder air-cooled radial piston engine
Maximum speed: 504km/h (313mph)

Range: 1006km (625 miles)
Ceiling: 10,000m (32,700ft)
Crew: 1
Armament: One 7.62mm (0.3in) M1919 and one 12.7mm (0.5in) M2 Browning machine guns fixed firing forward in upper front fuselage decking; some later aircraft fitted with an optional hardpoint under each wing

Opposite:
The olive drab and grey colour scheme of this P-36C was adopted by the USAAF for all its fighters in late 1941.

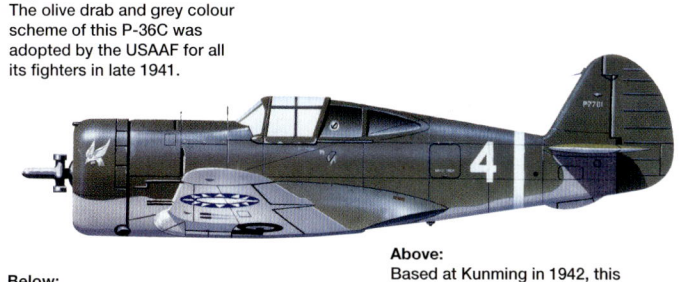

Below:
Flying with the 79th Pursuit Squadron, part of the 20th Pursuit Group, this P-36A was based at Moffett Field, California, in November 1939.

Above:
Based at Kunming in 1942, this Hawk 75A-5 was in service with Nationalist Chinese forces.

the Hawk 75 and obtained orders from Argentina, China and Thailand. France became the first export customer for the retractable-gear Hawk 75A and on 20 September 1939 an H75A-1 shot down a Messerschmitt Bf 109E, the first Allied air-to-air victory in the West. The Curtiss H75 proved to be the most successful fighter flown by France until the capitulation of June 1940, shooting down 311 aircraft, a third of all French victories.

Mohawk

French aircraft on order when France fell were diverted to the RAF, which named the aircraft the 'Mohawk', and it saw intense action with the RAF in Burma and India. Captured French H75s were supplied by Germany to Finland where the aircraft proved highly effective against Soviet aircraft and gained the nickname *Sussu* ('Sweetheart'). Although the P-36 saw little action with its country of origin, it did make history by attaining the first two US 'kills' of the war during the Pearl Harbor attack, shooting down a further three later that day. This would be the only occasion in which USAAF P-36s were flown in combat.

Curtiss P-40 Tomahawk

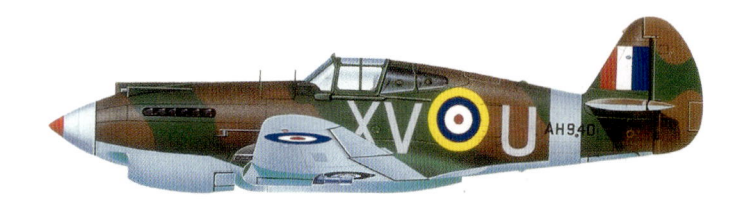

An inline engine development of the earlier radial-powered Hawk 75, the Curtiss Tomahawk was used in large numbers by Commonwealth forces, the USSR and the 'Flying Tigers'.

Essentially comprising a P-36 airframe mated to a V-12 Allison engine, the XP-40 flew for the first time on 14 October 1938 and by 1941 examples of the P-40B and C were stationed in Hawaii and the Philippines. When the Japanese attacked, the aircraft saw action in both locations but the vast majority of early P-40 use took place in the service of other nations. France ordered 230 P-40s but the RAF took

These Tomahawk Mk IIBs were serving with 112 Squadron, RAF, in the Western Desert, North Africa.

Curtiss Tomahawk Mk IB

Weight: 3655kg (8058lb)
Dimensions: Length 9.66m (31ft 9in), Wingspan 11.37m (37ft 4in), Height 3.22m (10ft 7in)
Powerplant: One 813kW (1090hp) Allison V-1710-33 V-12 liquid-cooled piston engine
Maximum speed: 555km/h (345mph)

Range: 1287km (800 miles)
Ceiling: 8990m (29,500ft)
Crew: 1
Armament: Two 12.7mm (0.5in) Colt Browning M2 machine guns fixed forward firing in fuselage nose; four 7.62mm (0.3in) Browning M1919 machine guns fixed forward firing in wings

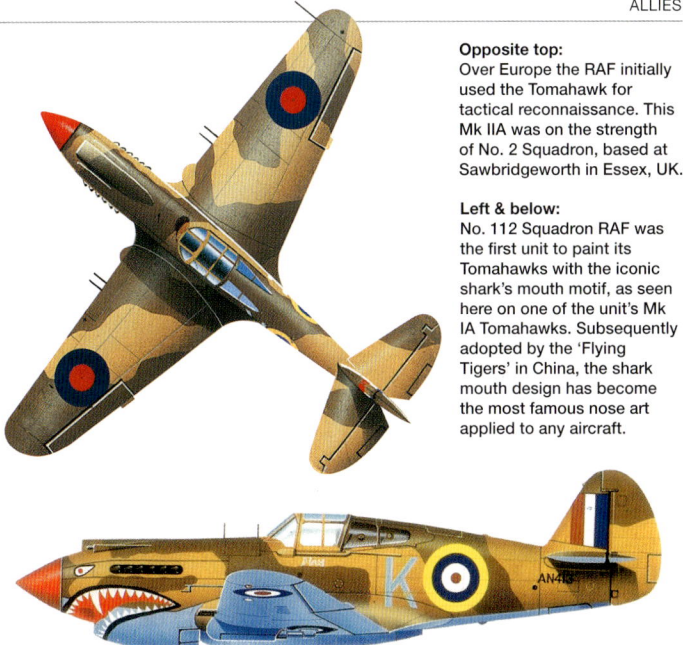

Opposite top:
Over Europe the RAF initially used the Tomahawk for tactical reconnaissance. This Mk IIA was on the strength of No. 2 Squadron, based at Sawbridgeworth in Essex, UK.

Left & below:
No. 112 Squadron RAF was the first unit to paint its Tomahawks with the iconic shark's mouth motif, as seen here on one of the unit's Mk IA Tomahawks. Subsequently adopted by the 'Flying Tigers' in China, the shark mouth design has become the most famous nose art applied to any aircraft.

over the order after the fall of France, giving the aircraft the name Tomahawk. The Tomahawk I was judged unsuitable by Fighter Command in Europe and was used for tactical reconnaissance instead but the remainder of the French order was delivered as the more combat-capable Tomahawk II that became the primary Commonwealth fighter type in Africa.

China service

RAF Tomahawk stocks were made available to other nations during 1941, the first recipient being China, which bought 100 examples for the American Volunteer Group (AVG), better known as the 'Flying Tigers'. Another recipient of many ex-RAF Tomahawks was the Soviet Union, with 195 Tomahawk IIBs sent from British stocks as military aid. Soviet Tomahawks were rushed into service, beginning combat operations in October 1941 over Moscow, and 17 kills were scored in the aircraft's first month of service.

Curtiss P-40 Kittyhawk

A relatively modest update to the Tomahawk, later P-40s were built in greater numbers than the earlier aircraft and would see action with virtually all Allied air forces.

During 1940 Curtiss sought to improve the P-40 by fitting it with the more powerful Allison V-1710-39(F3R), which was shorter than earlier Allison engines and possessed a raised thrust line. The aircraft also received an enlarged radiator and a smaller volume fuselage. The changes were sufficiently minimal that production could begin rapidly and 560 aircraft, named Kittyhawk, were ordered for

A single Kittyhawk IV, nearest the camera, is joined by three Mk IIIs, all of 84 Squadron RAAF in late 1943.

Curtiss P-40N

Weight: 4018kg (8850lb)
Dimensions: Length 10.17m (33ft 4in), Wingspan 11.37m (37ft 4in), Height 3.76m (12ft 4in)
Powerplant: One 895kW (1200hp) Allison V-1710-81 V-12 liquid-cooled piston engine
Maximum speed: 560km/h (348mph)

Range (max external fuel): 2010km (1250 miles)
Ceiling: 9449m (31000ft)
Crew: 1
Armament: Four 12.7mm (0.5in) Browning machine guns; up to 317kg (700lb) bombload

Opposite:
Based at Cutella in the Abruzzo region of Italy in early 1944, this Kittyhawk Mk IV was serving with 112 Squadron.

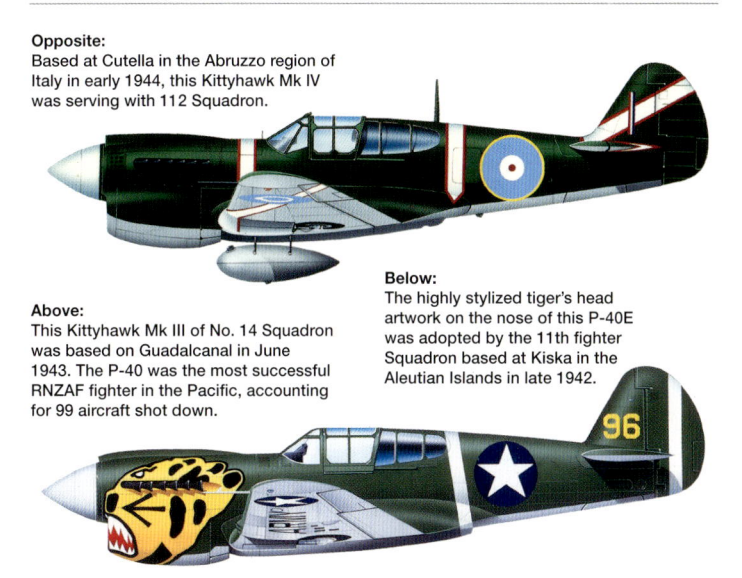

Above:
This Kittyhawk Mk III of No. 14 Squadron was based on Guadalcanal in June 1943. The P-40 was the most successful RNZAF fighter in the Pacific, accounting for 99 aircraft shot down.

Below:
The highly stylized tiger's head artwork on the nose of this P-40E was adopted by the 11th fighter Squadron based at Kiska in the Aleutian Islands in late 1942.

RAF service in May 1940, followed by the US in June. Initially used by the Royal Australian Air Force (RAAF) in New Guinea, Kittyhawks subsequently saw widespread service in North Africa and the Mediterranean where they were gradually adapted to perform fighter-bomber missions. This role suited the P-40, with its great structural strength and excellent speed and manoeuvrability at low altitude, but the aircraft's poor altitude performance prompted the production of the P-40F and L with the Packard Merlin.

P-40N

Further attempts to wring as much performance as possible out of the basic Allison-engined P-40 airframe resulted in the lightened P-40N, which was built in greater numbers than any other variant and was instantly identifiable by its much-improved and extended cockpit glazing. Comparatively little use was made of the P-40N by the US but most late production P-40s were intended purely for export anyway. Other major users of the Kittyhawk and later P-40s were the Soviet Union, Free France, Australia, Canada, the Netherlands, South Africa and New Zealand. Almost 14,000 P-40s of all variants were built in total.

Douglas P-70 Havoc

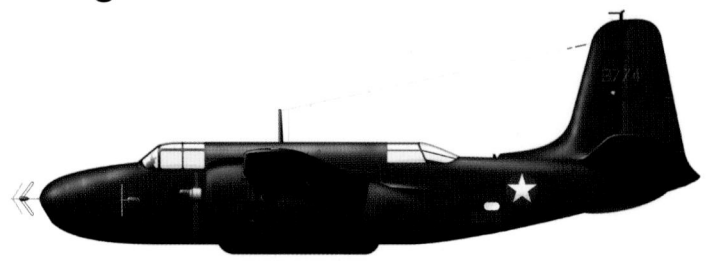

Although soon surpassed, the Douglas P-70 formed an important part of the UK and US's nocturnal fighter force when more effective aircraft were scarce.

Derived from the highly successful A-20 light bomber, the first night-fighter variants were developed in the United Kingdom for use by the RAF. The aircraft were the undelivered remainder of a French order for DB-7 attack aircraft, taken on by the British after the French capitulation, but the aircraft possessed far too short a range to be used effectively as bombers operating from UK bases

The arrowhead antenna of the British-developed SCR-540 radar can be seen on the nose of this P-70, the first US combat aircraft to carry airborne interception radar.

Douglas Havoc Mk II

Weight: 9654kg (21,264lb)
Dimensions: Length 14.5m (47ft 7in), Wingspan 18.69m (61ft 4in), Height 5.36m (17ft 7in)
Powerplant: Two 1177kW (1600hp) Wright R-2600-A5B Cyclone 14-cylinder air-cooled radial piston engines

Maximum speed: 529km/h (329mph)
Range: 1706km (1060 miles)
Ceiling: 8611m (28,250ft)
Crew: 2–3
Armament: None when equipped with Helmore Turbinlite; otherwise 12 7.7mm (0.303in) Browning machine guns fixed firing forward in nose

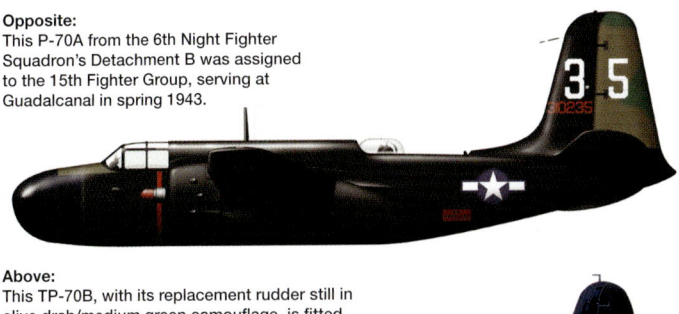

Opposite:
This P-70A from the 6th Night Fighter Squadron's Detachment B was assigned to the 15th Fighter Group, serving at Guadalcanal in spring 1943.

Above:
This TP-70B, with its replacement rudder still in olive drab/medium green camouflage, is fitted with American centimetric radar in the nose and is based on an A-20G airframe.

Above:
Douglas Havoc Mk I of 23 Squadron RAF, based at Ford in West Sussex, UK, in late 1941 for night intruder missions over Europe.

against targets in Europe, and the decision was taken to modify these aircraft into Havoc night fighters. These were fitted with flame-damping exhausts, an AI Mk IV or V radar set and a 'solid' nose containing eight (later 12) 7.7mm (0.303in) machine guns, though some Havocs retained the glazed nose and were fitted with four machine guns in the lower nose for night intruder missions from early 1941 onwards.

'Turbinlite'

Many Havocs were modified to carry the 2700 million candlepower Helmore/GEC searchlight, known as the 'Turbinlite', in the nose to illuminate enemy aircraft for an accompanying single-seat fighter to attack but this scheme proved impractical and achieved only a few successful interceptions. In the US, 59 of the first batch of A-20s on order were completed as P-70 night fighters. Although used primarily for training, a few were flown operationally in the Pacific and the type was responsible for the destruction of two Japanese aircraft.

Grumman F4F Wildcat/Martlet

The Wildcat was the most important Allied carrier fighter from 1940 until the appearance of the F6F Hellcat, seeing widespread service around the globe.

Despite losing to the Brewster F2A in the competition to supply the US Navy's first monoplane fighter, the F4F proved to be a hugely significant combat aircraft while the F2A lapsed into obscurity. Making its first flight on 2 September 1937, the F4F had originally been designed as a biplane but was modified into a monoplane before construction began. Before the aircraft entered US service, the F4F

An F4F-3 Wildcat of VF-6 takes off from USS *Enterprise* in the Coral Sea, May 1942.

Grumman F4F-4 Wildcat

Weight (maximum takeoff): 3978kg (8762lb)
Dimensions: Length 8.85m (29ft), Wingspan 11.59m (38ft), Height 3.44m (11ft 4in)
Powerplant: One 895kW (1200hp) Pratt & Whitney R-1830-86 Twin Wasp 14-cylinder air cooled radial piston engine
Speed: 515km/h (320mph)

Range: 2051km (1275 miles) with external tanks
Ceiling: 10,370m (34,000ft)
Crew: 1
Armament: Six 12.7mm (0.5in) AN/M2 Browning machine guns fixed forward firing in wings; up to 90kg (200lb) bombload under wings

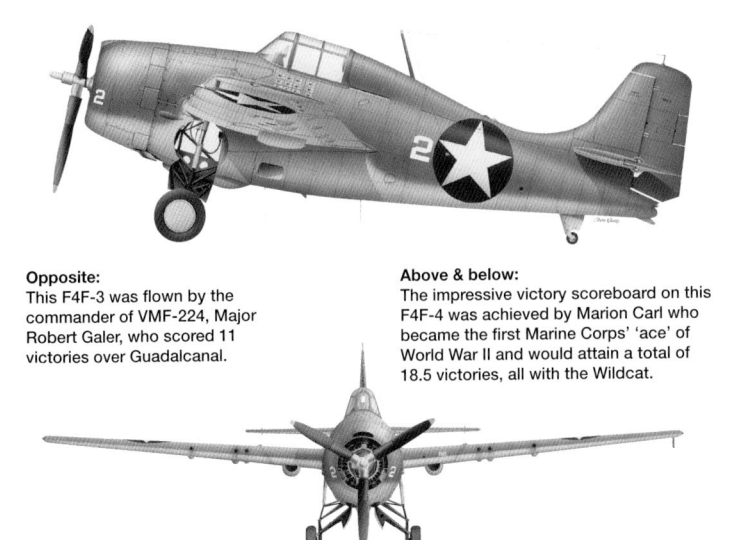

Opposite:
This F4F-3 was flown by the commander of VMF-224, Major Robert Galer, who scored 11 victories over Guadalcanal.

Above & below:
The impressive victory scoreboard on this F4F-4 was achieved by Marion Carl who became the first Marine Corps' 'ace' of World War II and would attain a total of 18.5 victories, all with the Wildcat.

had already seen action: Royal Navy examples (until 1944 named Martlet by the British) became the first American-designed aircraft to attain a victory by shooting down a Ju 88 on Christmas Day 1940. When the US entered the war, 245 Wildcats were on strength and the F4F was immediately in action in the defence of Wake Island, achieving its first combat victories in US service in the process.

Robust interceptor

Against its primary opponent, the A6M Zero, the Wildcat was at a speed disadvantage and the sprightly Zero was considerably more manoeuvrable, especially at lower speeds, though the F4F was much more robust. Later variants were built by General Motors (as the FM-1 and -2) and even after later carrier fighters appeared, the Wildcat remained useful due to its excellent deck take-off and landing characteristics that enabled it to operate from even the smallest escort carriers. In total 7860 Wildcats were produced, of which 4400 were FM-2s.

Grumman F6F Hellcat

Credited with more combat victories than any other naval fighter in history, the F6F Hellcat combined decent performance, easy deck landing characteristics and an immensely strong airframe.

Procured, presciently, as a back-up in the event of problems with the F4U Corsair, Grumman's replacement for the F4F enjoyed remarkably smooth development and flight testing following its first flight on 26 June 1942. The most significant change made before production began was a switch to the powerful and reliable Pratt & Whitney R-2800 Double Wasp in the second prototype. Initial

Pictured during deck landing training, the Deck Landing Officer is signalling the crew to remove the chocks from the wheels of this F6F-3.

Grumman F6F-5 Hellcat

Weight: 6002kg (13,221lb)
Dimensions: Length 10.17m (33ft 4in), Wingspan 13.08m (42ft 10in), Height 4.4m (14ft 5in)
Powerplant: One 1470kW (2000hp) Pratt & Whitney R-2800-10 Double Wasp two row 18-cylinder air cooled radial piston engine

Speed: 600km/h (373mph)
Range: 2606km (1620 miles) with external fuel tank
Ceiling: 11,438m (37,s500ft)
Crew: 1
Armament: Six 12.7mm (0.5in) Browning AN/M2 machine guns fixed forward firing in wings

Above:
During April 1944, this F6F-3 of VF-16 was serving aboard USS *Lexington*. This aircraft was flown by 7.5 victory ace Frank Fleming.

Opposite:
F6F-3 of VF-44, flying from USS *Langley* in October 1944 during the Battle of the Sibuyan Sea.

Above:
This US Navy F6F Hellcat served with VF-29.

deliveries began in January 1943, and the first Hellcats embarked on USS *Essex* during the spring of that year. Hellcats from USS *Yorktown* engaged in combat for the first time during August 1943, attacking Japanese positions on Marcus Island. Subsequently the F6F would fight in all major USN operations with the highpoint of its career likely being the Battle of the Philippine Sea of June 1944 when F6Fs shot down 243 Japanese aircraft, an action which would become known as the 'Marianas Turkey Shoot', effectively ending the ability of the Imperial Japanese Navy to conduct carrier operations.

Royal Navy Hellcats

The British Royal Navy also used large numbers of Hellcats, initially using them to conduct anti-shipping missions along the Norwegian coast but, like their US counterparts, the majority of British Hellcat operations would take place in the Pacific. In total 12,275 Hellcats were built and an unprecedented 305 US flyers became aces with five or more 'kills' with the type, more than in any other US aircraft.

Lockheed P-38 Lightning

Initially schemed as a high-speed interceptor to complement the P-39 Airacobra, the P-38 Lightning was highly unconventional but proved hugely successful.

The P-38 was designed in contravention to prevailing Air Corps orthodoxy, being intended from the start to possess excellent high-altitude performance, long range and a heavy installed armament. First flown on 27 January 1939, the aircraft was of radical design and boasted terrific performance. The XP-38 prototype set a new transcontinental speed record when it flew from California to New

A factory-fresh P-38H flies over Lockheed's Burbank facility, California, prior to delivery to the USAAF.

Lockheed P-38F

Weight: 9798kg (21,600lb)
Dimensions: Length 1.53m (37ft 10in), Wingspan 15.85m (52ft), Height 3.91m (12ft 10in)
Powerplant: Two 913kW (1225hp) Allison V-1710-49 left-hand rotation and -53 right-hand rotation V-12 liquid-cooled piston engines

Maximum speed: 628km/h (390mph)
Range: 1126km (700 miles)
Ceiling: 11,582m (38,000ft)
Crew: 1
Armament: One 20mm (0.79in) Hispano cannon and four 12.7mm (0.5in) Browning M2 machine guns fixed forward firing in nose

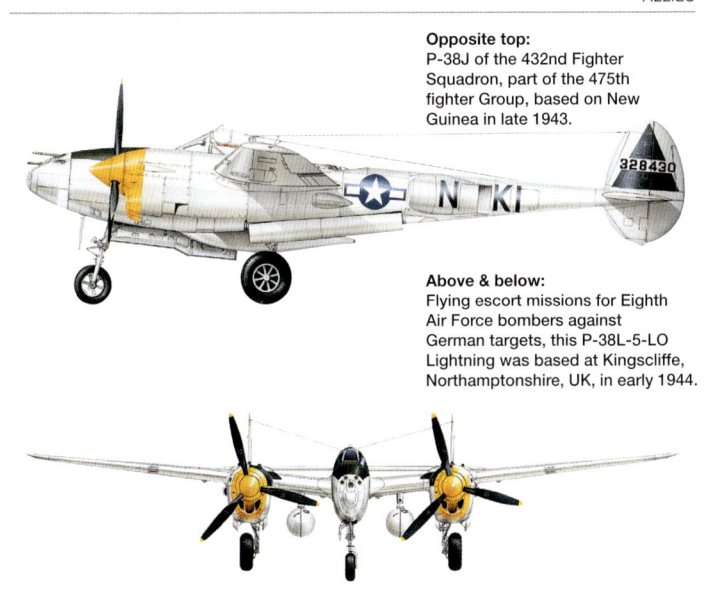

Opposite top:
P-38J of the 432nd Fighter Squadron, part of the 475th fighter Group, based on New Guinea in late 1943.

Above & below:
Flying escort missions for Eighth Air Force bombers against German targets, this P-38L-5-LO Lightning was based at Kingscliffe, Northamptonshire, UK, in early 1944.

York at an average speed of 563km/h (350mph). Production aircraft entered service in July 1941 and the first Lightning victory occurred on 4 August 1942 when two Alaska-based P-38s shot down two Kawanishi H6K flying boats. At roughly the same time, the first P-38s arrived in Europe and the Lightning's first *Luftwaffe* victim, an Fw 200, was shot down on 15 August.

Escort role

Engaged primarily in escort work, the P-38 initially suffered heavy losses. This improved over time but like all 'heavy' fighters such as the Bf 110 and Ki-45, the Lightning was at a disadvantage when dealing with modern single-engine fighters. As the P-47 and particularly the P-51 became available, the P-38 switched to a successful secondary career in a fighter-bomber role. In the Pacific the Lightning proved effective as long range was of paramount importance and the security afforded by two engines was appreciated by pilots. The P-38 achieved the longest distance interception mission of the entire war when P-38Gs shot down the G4M bomber carrying Admiral Isoroku Yamamoto after an overwater flight of 700km (435 miles).

Lockheed P-80 Shooting Star

The first American jet fighter to see active service, the P-80 was developed very quickly and entered service before the end of the war in Europe, though only just.

The first American jet aircraft, the Bell P-59 Airacomet, had proven to be a decent research aircraft and was useful for introducing the first jet pilots to this novel new form of power. However, it was clear that the performance of the P-59 was insufficient for active service and the development of a new jet fighter was assigned the utmost priority. Lockheed promised they could

The first official USAF display team was the 'Acrojets', flying the P-80A and based at Fighter School at Williams AFB, 1948.

Lockheed P-80A Shooting Star

Weight: 6356kg (14,000lb)
Dimensions: Length 10.51m (34ft 6in), Wingspan 11.85m (38ft 10in), Height 3.45m (11ft 4in)
Powerplant: One 1746kg (3850lb) static thrust General Electric J33-GE-9 centrifugal flow turbojet engine
Maximum speed: 898km/h (558mph)

Range (with two drop tanks): 1770km (1100 miles)
Ceiling: 13,716m (45,000ft)
Crew: 1
Armament: Six 12.7mm (0.5in) Colt Browning M2 machine guns fixed forward firing in nose; up to 908kg (2000lb) bombload or 10 12.7cm (5in) rockets under wings

construct a prototype within 150 days, meeting this target with seven days to spare when the XP-80 was delivered to Muroc Airfield on 16 November 1943. Delays afflicted American engine production and thus the first XP-80A (named Lulu-Belle) was flown on 8 January 1944 powered by a British-built de Havilland Goblin.

YP-90A

This was followed on 13 September by the first of 12 service test YP-80As, by which time the engine had been changed to the Allison J33. The programme was beset with problems: test pilot Milo Burcham lost his life while flying the third YP-80A and his successor Tony LeVier suffered a broken back after bailing out of a stricken Shooting Star. Despite the setbacks, four pre-production YP-80As were sent to Europe for operational testing and two of the Shooting Stars performed operational reconnaissance missions in Italy during February and March 1945. In total 1715 P-80s were built and in Korea a Shooting Star was downed by a MiG-15 in the world's first jet versus jet aerial combat.

North American P-51/A-36 Mustang (Allison V-1710-powered variants)

The Mustang owed its existence to a British requirement and early examples, while demonstrating outstanding speed and handling at low level, were poor high-altitude performers.

In 1939, the British Purchasing Commission approached North American Aviation Inc with the suggestion that the company build Curtiss P-40s for the RAF. Manager 'Dutch' Kindelberger proposed instead that they design a better aircraft, even though North American had never built a fighter before. Nonetheless the British gave the go-ahead and the prototype was built in 102 days, and

The A-36A was an attack aircraft variant of the famed P-51 Mustang fighter but was actually in service before the P-51.

North American P-51A Mustang

Weight: 4808kg (10,600lb)
Dimensions: Length 9.83m (32ft 3in), Wingspan 11.28m (37ft), Height 3.71m (12ft 2in)
Powerplant: One 895kW (1200hp) Allison V-1710-81 V-12 liquid-cooled piston engine
Maximum speed: 628km/h (390mph)

Range: 2011km (1250 miles)
Ceiling: 9555m (31,350ft)
Crew: 1
Armament: Four 12.7mm (0.5in) Browning M2 machine guns fixed forward firing in wings; up to 454kg (1000lb) bombload; modification in field to permit carriage of three rocket launch tubes under each wing

Opposite:
The A-36A was an attack aircraft variant of the famed P-51 Mustang fighter but was actually in service before the P-51. The A-36A shared the Mustang's airframe but never had the upgrade to the Rolls-Royce Merlin engine.

Below (both images):
AM101, the 364th Mustang I built for the UK, commenced operations with No. 26 Sqn from RAF Gatwick in January 1942.

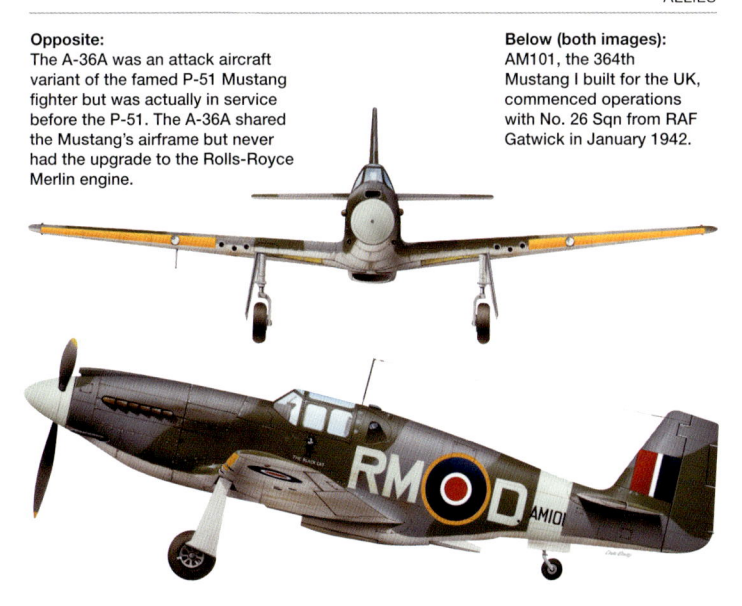

despite the engine being delayed, the NA-73X flew on 26 October 1940. Testing of the Mustang Mk I in the UK revealed the excellence of the design, described as the best fighter aircraft so far received from the USA. Speed, handling and manoeuvrability were all excellent, though performance rapidly diminished at altitudes above around 3965m (13,000ft) due to the Allison V-1710 engine's lack of a two-stage supercharger. As most aerial combat over Western Europe took place above that altitude, it was decided that the aircraft would be ideal for the tactical reconnaissance role.

Tactical reconnaissance

One of these aircraft scored the type's first victory on 19 August 1942, shooting down an Fw 190 over Dieppe. So effective was the Mustang in the low-level role that the RAF retained the aircraft in service until the conclusion of hostilities. The USAAF used the early Mustang as a reconnaissance platform but also utilized it as a dive-bomber in North Africa and Italy, designated the A-36, and as a fighter in Asia, escorting B-24 and B-25 raids in Burma.

North American P-51 Mustang

(Packard V-1650 Merlin-powered variants)

The marriage of the Merlin engine to the Mustang airframe resulted in the finest American fighter of the war, arguably the most successful piston-engined fighter in history.

The idea of fitting the Merlin to the Mustang originated with Rolls-Royce test pilot Ronnie Harker and trial conversions were made virtually simultaneously in the UK and US. The results were impressive with the aircraft demonstrating a rate of climb nearly double that of the Allison-powered aircraft and well over 100km/h (60mph) faster. Altitude performance was transformed and

P-51s destined for the RAF were tested in the US in British camouflage but US markings with the addition of an RAF fin flash as seen on this Mustang Mk III.

North American P-51D Mustang

Weight: 5493kg (12,100lb)
Dimensions: Length 9.83m (32ft 3in), Wingspan 11.28m (37ft), Height 4.16m (13ft 8in)
Powerplant: One 1264kW (1695hp) piston engine
Maximum speed: 703km/h (437mph)
Range (with external fuel): 2655km (1650 miles)

Ceiling: 12,800 m (42,000ft)
Crew: 1
Armament: Six 12.7mm (0.5in) Browning M2 machine guns fixed forward firing in wings; up to 908kg (2000lb) bombload; later production aircraft fitted with provision for three rocket launch tubes under each wing

Opposite:
Ralph 'Doc' Watson, a five-victory ace, flew this P-51D with the 52nd FG, part of the 15th Air Force based in southern Italy.

Above:
This P-51B 'Beantown Banshee' was flown by Felix M Rogers in early 1944.

Below:
Based at Leiston, Suffolk, UK, this P-51K 'Nooky Booky IV' was the personal aircraft of Leonard 'Kit' Carson.

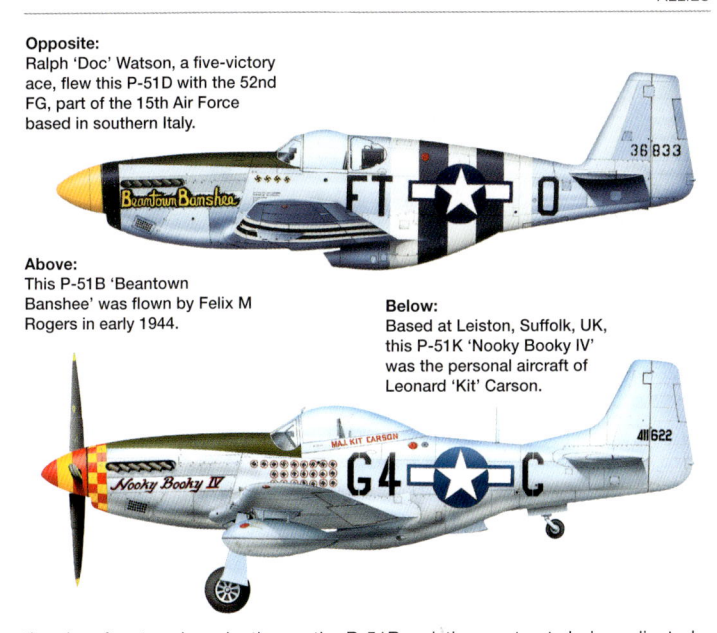

the aircraft entered production as the P-51B, existing contracts being adjusted to cover Merlin-powered aircraft. With drop tanks fitted, the Mustang offered a range comfortably in excess of that achievable by either the P-47 Thunderbolt or P-38 Lightning and was a more manoeuvrable aircraft than either of them.

Bomber escort

The early months of 1944 saw the first use of the P-51 as a bomber escort over Europe, though initially these operations were plagued with teething mechanical troubles. By 4 March, however, P-51s became the first Allied single-engine fighters to fly over Berlin and the aircraft spearheaded the systematic destruction of the *Luftwaffe* as a viable fighting force. Although some ground attack work was carried out as aerial opposition dwindled, the P-51 was primarily a pure escort fighter and undertook the same duties in the Pacific, flying its first B-29 escort mission, to Tokyo, on 7 April 1945. Large numbers were also supplied to the RAF and the Mustang served with over 25 air forces postwar.

Northrop P-61 Black Widow

Northrop's first combat aircraft design and the world's first fighter specifically designed to carry radar, the P-61 was of a size and weight more akin to a medium bomber.

Initially designed to a British requirement, the P-61 was the first purpose-built night fighter of the war and would become the largest and heaviest fighter to see service during the conflict. The first XP-61 was completed in the early spring of 1942 and the first flight was made with a mock-up of the remotely controlled dorsal turret, the actual turret being delayed due to the B-29,

Initially P-61s were finished in olive drab as seen here, before the more appropriate overall gloss black finish was adopted.

Northrop P-61B Black Widow

Weight: 16,420kg (36,200lb)
Dimensions: Length 15.11m (49ft 7in), Wingspan 20.12m (66ft), Height 4.47m (14ft 8in)
Powerplant: Two 1,680kW (2,250hp) Pratt & Whitney R-2800-65W Double Wasp 18-cylinder air-cooled radial piston engines
Maximum speed: 589km/h (366mph)
Range: 2170km (1350 miles)

Ceiling: 10,100m (33,100ft)
Crew: 3
Armament: Four 20mm (0.79in) Hispano AN/M2 cannon fixed forward firing in ventral fuselage and four 12.7mm (0.5in) M2 Browning machine guns in remotely operated upper turret; underwing racks for bombs up to 726kg (1600lb) each

Opposite:
'Jukin Judy' shows the form in which the P-61 first went into action, devoid of the troublesome dorsal turret. This aircraft was based at Scorton, North Yorkshire, UK, in late 1944.

Above & below:
This P-61B, named 'Time's A Wastin', was based at McGuire Field, Mindoro, Philippines, in January 1945. The P-51B reintroduced the dorsal turret and introduced a swathe of other changes including the addition of four external pylons.

which utilized the same turret design, having priority. Subsequently, problems with buffeting caused by the turret saw the first 200 P-61s completed without this feature. Other delays also occurred, primarily due to the flying controls; unusually the P-61 utilized spoilers for primary lateral control and, once perfected, this system gave the aircraft surprisingly good manoeuvrability for its size.

Pacific operations

Initial P-61 operations took place in May 1944, with the 9th Air Force based in England. The first P-61s arrived in the Pacific in the following month and it was here that the type achieved its first victory, when a Mitsubishi G3M was shot down on 30 June. The ongoing reduction in enemy air activity meant further nocturnal victories in both theatres dwindled and the P-61 was used both as a night intruder and for daylight ground attack missions.

Republic P-47 Thunderbolt

The P-47 was the heaviest single-engine fighter of World War II. A more versatile aircraft than the more famous P-51, the Thunderbolt was built in greater numbers.

Designed by Georgian emigré Alexander Kartveli, the prototype Thunderbolt flew for the first time on 6 May 1941 and benefitted from aerial combat reports coming out of Europe. As a result, the installed armament of eight 12.7mm (0.5in) machine guns, all in the wings, was considerably heavier than the norm for contemporary American fighters and from the start the aircraft was protected

The final wartime variant was the formidable P-47N with its new wing.

Republic P-47D

Weight: 7938kg (17,500lb)
Dimensions: Length 10.99m (36ft 1in), Wingspan 12.43m (40ft 9in), Height 4.44m (14ft 7in)
Powerplant: One 1500kW (2000hp) Pratt & Whitney R-2800-59 18-cylinder air-cooled radial piston engine
Speed: 686km/h (426mph)

Range (with external fuel): 1660km (1030 miles)
Ceiling: 13,000m (42,000ft)
Crew: 1
Armament: Eight 12.7mm (0.5in) M2 Browning machine guns; up to 1100kg (2500lb) of bombs or six zero-length rockets under wings with drop tanks or 10 rockets without drop tanks

Opposite:
This P-47C was based at Debden, Essex, UK, in March 1943. It was serving with the 334th Fighter Squadron, 4th Fighter Group.

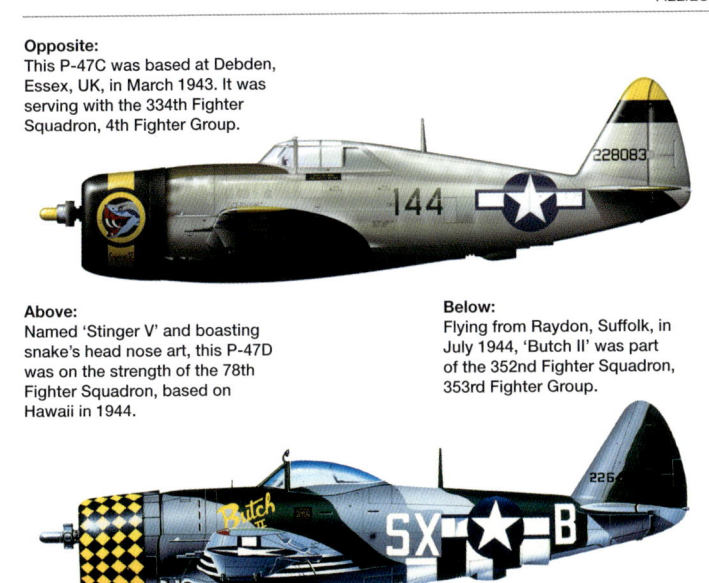

Above:
Named 'Stinger V' and boasting snake's head nose art, this P-47D was on the strength of the 78th Fighter Squadron, based on Hawaii in 1944.

Below:
Flying from Raydon, Suffolk, in July 1944, 'Butch II' was part of the 352nd Fighter Squadron, 353rd Fighter Group.

with self-sealing fuel tanks and armour. The higher than expected altitudes at which fighter combat was taking place over Europe had also been noted and a General Electric turbo-supercharger was fitted in the rear fuselage. The first operational missions were flown in Europe during March 1943 and initial use centred on escorting daylight heavy bombing raids.

Ground-attack role

As the longer-ranged P-51 increasingly took over the escort role, the P-47 began a highly effective second career as a fighter-bomber, becoming the most successful US ground attack aircraft of the war. Later P-47s adopted a clear view bubble canopy and later still the P-47N, arguably the best all-round Allied fighter of the war, carried a colossal fuel load giving it a maximum range of some 3781km (2350 miles) and boasted a 740km/h (460mph) top speed, a superior range and performance to the much-vaunted P-51D Mustang. However, the P-47N only entered service in April 1945 and operated exclusively in the Pacific.

Vought F4U Corsair

One of the most successful combat aircraft in history, the F4U overcame its reputation as a tricky handling aircraft to achieve the longest production run of any US piston-engined fighter.

Designed by Rex Beisel, the prototype F4U flew on 29 May 1939 and gained early fame by becoming the first US fighter to exceed 650km/h (400mph) in level flight. Early in its career the F4U developed a reputation as difficult to deck-land, especially compared to the docile F6F Hellcat, and this influenced the decision, taken primarily for logistical reasons, to standardize on the F6F for the US Navy's carrier

F4Us crowd the flight deck of USS *Bunker Hill*. The Corsair only began to regularly operate from US carriers in 1944.

Vought F4U-1A Corsair

Weight (maximum takeoff): 6350kg (14,000lb)
Dimensions: Length 10.16m (33ft 4in), Wingspan 12.5m (41ft), Height 5.13m (16ft 10in)
Powerplant: One 1770kW (2380hp) Pratt & Whitney R-2800-8 Double Wasp 14-cylinder air-cooled radial piston engine

Speed: 671km/h (417mph)
Range: 1633km (1015 miles)
Ceiling: 11,247m (36,900ft)
Crew: 1
Armament: Six 12.7mm (0.50in) M2 Browning machine guns fixed forward firing in wings

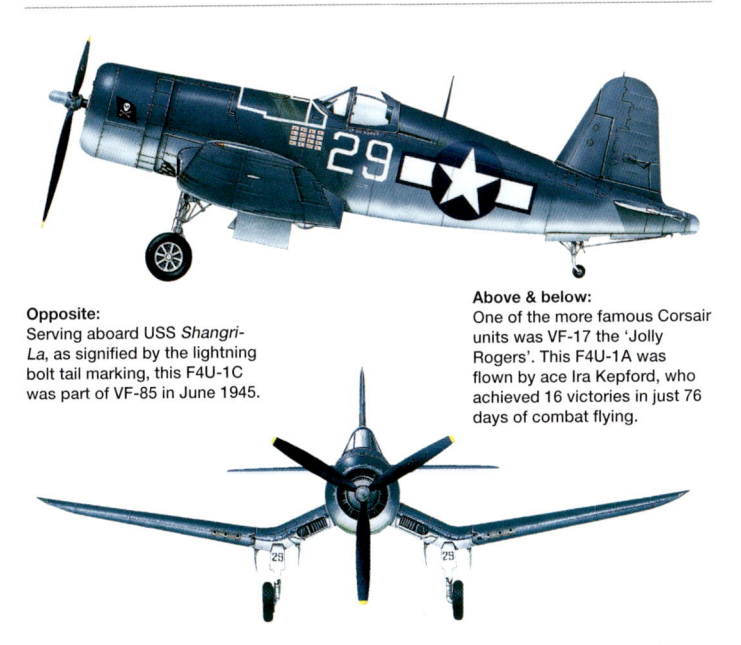

Opposite:
Serving aboard USS *Shangri-La*, as signified by the lightning bolt tail marking, this F4U-1C was part of VF-85 in June 1945.

Above & below:
One of the more famous Corsair units was VF-17 the 'Jolly Rogers'. This F4U-1A was flown by ace Ira Kepford, who achieved 16 victories in just 76 days of combat flying.

fighter and supply the F4U to Marine Corps units flying from shore bases. The Corsair's performance in the air was not in any doubt, however, and it proved devastatingly effective in combat. The highest scoring F4U 'ace' was Kenneth Walsh who shot down 21 aircraft with the Vought fighter.

Royal Navy service
The Royal Navy also became an enthusiastic F4U operator, flying it from carriers from mid 1943 and using it in action in both Europe and the Pacific. Royal Navy Corsairs were instantly identifiable as they required 22cm (8in) clipped from each wingtip to allow the aircraft to fit within the cramped hangars of British carriers. Vought worked hard to improve the Corsair's deck-landing characteristics and following improvements, the aircraft began flying from USN carriers from early 1944. The F4U proved more amenable to ground attack tasks than the Hellcat, this eventually becoming the primary role of the aircraft, and F4Us operated as fighter-bombers throughout the Korean War.

Rogožarski IK-3

The majority of Yugoslavia's fighter inventory consisted of foreign aircraft but domestic manufacturer Rogožarski produced the IK-3, which saw brief but furious action in April 1941.

Yugoslavia had already built a fighter aircraft in the form of the Ikarus IK-2, a gull wing strut-braced monoplane redolent of the PZL P.11, 12 of which were built, but the IK-3 was much more advanced, featuring retractable undercarriage and a high projected performance. The design was the brainchild of two engineers, Ljubomir Ilic and Kosta Sivcev, who initially developed the aircraft privately before

A Yugoslav Air Force Rogožarski IK-2 parked in an unidentified field.

Rogožarski IK-3

Weight: 2630kg (5798lb)
Dimensions: Length 8m (26ft 3in), Wingspan 10.3m (33ft 10in), Height 3.25m (10ft 8in)
Powerplant: One 730kW (980hp) Avia 12Ycrs (licence-built Hispano Suiza 12Ycrs) V-12 liquid-cooled piston engine
Maximum speed: 527km/h (327mph)

Range: 785km (488 miles)
Ceiling: 9400m (30,800ft)
Crew: 1
Armament: One Oerlikon FF 20mm (0.8in) cannon firing through the propeller hub and two 7.92mm (0.312in) Browning/FN machine guns in the fuselage nose

Opposite & right:
The influence of the Hawker Hurricane on the design of the IK-3 is apparent. This example served with the 51st Independent Fighter Group of the 6th Fighter Regiment based at Zemun, near Belgrade, in April 1941.

Right: Pilots of the 51st Group, 6th Fighter Regiment, stand in front of an IK-3 fighter, Belgrade 1940.

approaching the VVKJ, *Vazduhoplovstvo vojske Kraljevine Jugoslavije* (Royal Yugoslavian Air Force). The Rogožarski A.D. company was selected to build the aircraft and the first flight occurred in May 1938. Tested against a VVKJ Bf 109E, the IK-3 was found to be somewhat slower but outmanoeuvred the Messerschmitt with ease. The programme was delayed due to the loss of the prototype after it disintegrated in flight and, although the accident was attributed to pilot error, production aircraft had a strengthened structure.

IK-3 in action

Only 12 aircraft were completed, mainly due to difficulties in obtaining further Hispano-Suiza 12Y engines, and further development of the IK-3 powered by either the Rolls-Royce Merlin or Daimler-Benz DB 601 was being undertaken when Yugoslavia was invaded by Germany, Italy and Hungary. During 11 days of fighting the IK-3s shot down 11 aircraft, four of them by Milislav Semiz, the top-scoring IK-3 pilot.

Axis

German technological prowess was regarded with respect during the war and the remarkably successful Messerschmitt Bf 109 tended to be the benchmark against which other fighters were judged, especially in the early war period. The German introduction of the first jets in large numbers only enhanced this reputation among their foes. Italy by contrast produced some outstanding designs but never had the industrial capacity to build enough of them before the armistice of 1943. Japan, meanwhile, pursued a unique course in fighter design philosophy, stressing agility as paramount over every other design attribute, leading to a succession of outstandingly manoeuvrable but excessively lightweight fighters.

Opposite: The archetypal German fighter was the Bf 109, which fought from the first day of the European war to the last, though ultimately over 35,000 of them were not enough to prevent Germany's defeat. These brand new Bf 109G-2s were lined up ready for test flying at Messerschmitt's Prüfening Aircraft Assembly Plant, Regensburg, in July 1942.

Avia B.534

One of the best combat biplanes ever built, the elegant B.534 was likely the finest fighter in the world when it entered service in 1933.

Sadly for Avia, the 1930s were a time of intensely rapid military aviation development and the B.534 was obsolete by the time Germany annexed Czechoslovakia in 1938. Despite this, the aircraft enjoyed a long career in a variety of roles. As well as the standard fighter armed with four machine guns on the fuselage sides, the Bk.534 variant deleted two of the fuselage machine guns but

B.534s were produced in four series. Earlier examples such as this one featured open cockpits and wooden propellers.

Avia B.534-IV

Weight: 1980kg (4365lb)
Dimensions: Length 8.1m (26ft 7in), Wingspan 9.4m (30ft 10in), Height 3.15m (10ft 4in)
Powerplant: One Hispano-Suiza 12Ydrs liquid-cooled V12 piston engine, 633kW (849hp)
Maximum speed: 405km/h (252mph)

Range: 600km (370 miles)
Ceiling: 10,600m (34,800ft)
Crew: 1
Armament: Four 7.92mm (0.31in) Letecky kulomet vz. 30 machine guns; up to 80kg (176lb) bombload

Opposite:
An example of the second production series, this B.534. II served with the 31st Fighter Squadron, Air Regiment 1, at Hradec Kralove, northern Czechoslovakia, in May 1938.

Above & right:
Fourth series B.534s featured an enclosed cockpit and light alloy propeller. This B.534.IV was with the Royal Bulgarian Air Force in 1942; Bulgarian aircraft were used to intercept USAAF B-24s en route to bomb the Ploiesti oil refinery.

added a 20mm (0.79in) gun firing through the propeller spinner. Later production aircraft featured a cut-down rear fuselage and rear cockpit glazing allowing for a 360-degree view from the cockpit.

Slovak fighter

Both B.534 and Bk.534s served with Slovak fighter units on the Eastern Front and achieved a few victories over Soviet aircraft during September 1941. However, three examples fell into the hands of the Slovak National Uprising of 1944, one of which shot down a Hungarian Ju-52/3m, believed to be the last air-to-air victory achieved by a biplane fighter. Germany also utilized the B.534 as an advanced trainer, glider and target tug, as well as testing it with an arrester hook as a potential naval fighter for their planned carrier, *Graf Zeppelin*. Bulgaria, Greece and Yugoslavia all also operated B.534s in the fighter role.

Arado Ar 240

Featuring a swathe of advanced design features, the Ar 240 was never ordered into mass production but was nonetheless utilized in operational service.

Built to a 1938 specification calling for a heavy fighter to replace the Messerschmitt Bf 110 which had recently entered service, the Ar 240 ambitiously combined a technically advanced remote-control defensive gun system, cockpit pressurization, ducted spinners directing air to annular radiators behind each propeller, and an unusually small wing for an aircraft of its size and weight,

This is the fifth prototype Ar 240 which was issued to the reconnaissance unit 1.(F)/Aufkl. Gr. Ob.d.L. in early 1942 for operational trials over Russia.

Arado Ar 240A-01

Weight: 10,297kg (22,701lb)
Dimensions: Length 12.81m (42ft 0in), Wingspan 13.34m (43ft 9in), Height 3.95m (13ft 0in)
Powerplant: Two 876kW (1175hp) Daimler-Benz DB 601E inverted V-12 liquid-cooled piston engines
Maximum speed: 618km/h (384mph)

Range: 2000km (1200 miles)
Ceiling: 10,500m (34,400ft)
Crew: 2
Armament: Two 7.92mm (0.31in) MG 17 machine guns fixed in the wing roots, one dorsal and one ventral remote-control turret with two 7.92mm (0.31in) MG 81 machine guns flexibly mounted in each

Opposite top:
The second Ar 240A pre-production aircraft was completed by September 1942 and wears the badge of the *Aufklärungsgruppe Oberbefehlshaber der Luftwaffe* reconnaissance unit on the nose.

Above:
Fitted with Lichtenstein air interception radar, the Ar 240 night-fighter variant was flown in late 1943 but never entered operational service.

The Arado 240C-1 was the heavy fighter version of the type.

leading to a wing loading nearly double that of the Bf 110. The small wing was adopted to minimize drag and the company had developed the 'Arado travelling flap' which greatly increased lift at low speeds.

Dive-bomber
The German fascination with dive-bombing also saw the Ar 240 fitted with a distinctive dive brake behind the tailplane. Only 15 Ar 240s were built due to the aircraft's persistent stability problems. The engines were also prone to overheating, leading to the unique expedient of fitting auxiliary radiators to the undercarriage legs, increasing cooling when the wheels were lowered. Although the technical issues precluded mass production going ahead, the Ar 240's performance saw it undertake the dangerous task of penetrating British airspace by daylight in the reconnaissance role, which by 1942 was effectively off limits to any other German reconnaissance aircraft. A few examples also saw operational service in Finland and on the Eastern Front.

Dornier Do 17 and Do 215

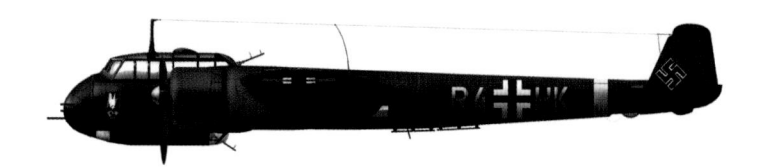

> The Do 17 came to be utilized as a night fighter largely due to the availability of surplus airframes as the aircraft was withdrawn from its primary role as a frontline bomber.

The beginning of the nocturnal RAF bombing campaign against German targets began in May 1940 and saw the *Luftwaffe* scramble to create a night-fighter arm to defend against these attacks. Initially equipped with Bf 110 and Ju 88s, other aircraft types were considered and the first three Do 17 fighter conversions, named *Kauz* ('Screech Owl'), consisted of a Ju 88C-2 nose grafted onto a Do 17Z but

Widely used as a bomber, the Do 17's performance was adequate for the night-fighter role. These are Do 17Z-2 bombers with the Croat-manned 15.(Kroat)/KG 53.

Dornier Do 215B-5 *Kauz III*

Weight: 6800kg (14,991lb)
Dimensions: Length 15.8m (51ft 10in), Wingspan 18m (59ft 1in), Height 4.56m (15ft)
Powerplant: Two 802kW (1075hp) Daimler-Benz DB 601A inverted V-12 liquid-cooled piston engines
Speed: 470km/h (290mph)

Range: 380km (240 miles)
Ceiling: 9000m (30,000ft)
Crew: 3
Armament: Two 20mm (0.79in) MG FF cannon and four 7.92mm (0.31in) MG 17 machine guns in nose, one flexibly mounted 7.92mm (0.31in) MG 17 machine gun in rear cockpit

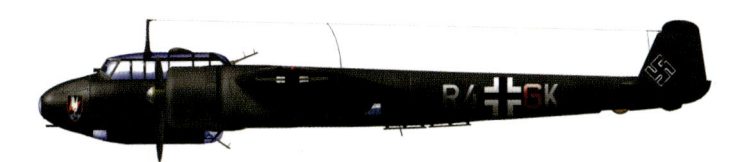

Opposite:
I./NJG2 performed night-intruder operations over the British Isles in 1940 and 1941. This aircraft was heavily damaged by flak but managed to crash land at its home base of Gilze Rijen, the Netherlands, in October 1940.

Above:
Another I./NJG2 aircraft, this Do 17Z-10 *Kauz*, also based at Gilze Rijen, features the troublesome *Spanner Anlage* infrared detection system, intended to detect aircraft engine exhausts in the nose.

Above:
This Do 215B-5 *Kauz* III of Stab II/ NJG 2 was based at Leeuwarden in the summer of 1942.

proved unsatisfactory. *Kauz II,* however, featured a new purpose-designed nose incorporating the *Spanner Anlage* infrared detection system plus two MG FF cannon and four MG 17 machine guns, and 10 *Kauz II* conversions were built.

First victory

The type scored its first victory on the night of 16/17 October 1940, which was also the first interception in which ground radar had successfully guided a German fighter to its target. Further development centred around the Do 215, which had started life as an export variant of the Do 17 before being built in quantity for the *Luftwaffe.* The resultant Do 215 *Kauz III* conversion, of which 20 were produced, became the first Dornier night fighter to be fitted with radar, significantly improving its effectiveness, and it achieved its first victory on 8/9 August 1941.

Dornier Do 217

Dornier's twin-engine bomber series continued with the Do 217 which, like its forebears, was converted into a night fighter, though with much more success.

The *Luftwaffe* favoured the Bf 110 and Ju 88 for its night-fighter requirements but shortages of both these aircraft led to the Do 217 being considered for the role. The Do 217 was an enlarged development of the Do 215 possessing higher performance and although capable of carrying a very heavy armament, there were concerns about the aircraft's size and weight. The initial Do 217J-1, operational from

The nose of this Do 217N-2 was crammed with four cannon, four guns and the antennas of the FuG 212 C-1 radar unit.

Dornier Do 217N-1

Weight: 15,000kg (33,000lb)
Dimensions: Length 17.67m (57ft 11in), Wingspan 19m (62ft 4in), Height 4.8m (15ft 8in)
Powerplant: Two 1380kW (1850hp) Daimler-Benz DB 603A inverted V-12 liquid-cooled piston engines
Speed: 525km/h (326mph)
Range: 1755km (1090 miles)

Ceiling: 8400m (27,600ft)
Crew: 4
Armament: Four 20mm (0.79in) MG 151 cannon and four 7.92mm (0.31in) MG 17 machine guns in nose; one 13mm (0.51in) MG 131 machine gun in dorsal turret and one 7.92mm (0.31in) MG13 in ventral position

Opposite:
Still wearing its factory codes, this Do 217J-1 was undergoing flight testing in Germany early in 1943.

Above:
This Do 217J-1 wears the badge of *Nachtjagdgeschwader* 4 on the nose and features an overall black colour scheme.

Below:
Serving with 11./NJG 4, this Do 217N-1, powered by Daimler-Benz DB 603 inline engines rather than the radial BMW 801 of the Do 217J, was based at Mainz-Finthen in Germany.

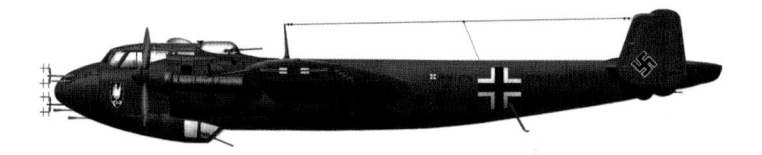

February 1942 and intended primarily as a nocturnal intruder, did not feature a radar and retained the bomb bay but carried the impressive armament of four 20mm (0.79in) cannon and four 7.92mm (0.31in) machine guns in the nose. The J-2, however, was intended as a night fighter from the start, equipped with *Lichtenstein* BC (FuG 202) radar and with the rear bomb bay blanked off.

Night fighter

The J-2's performance was disappointing due to its weight but it was used in the first *Schräge Musik* trial fittings. The Do 217N series was far more effective, especially the lightened Do 217N-2 which dispensed with the defensive turret and guns, trimming around two tonnes from the gross weight and greatly improving performance. Although it proved effective, most aircrew preferred the Bf 110 and Ju 88 and the Do 217 was withdrawn from operations by mid 1944.

Dornier Do 335

Featuring a push-pull configuration for its two engines, the Dornier Do 335 boasted exceptional performance but delays kept all but a handful of this impressive fighter from seeing service.

The main advantage of placing the engines of a twin in tandem is reduced drag, though this layout also allows for a better rate of roll and minimizes control problems if one engine should fail. Dornier had considerable experience with this engine arrangement but had not applied it to a high-performance fighter before and the Do 335 required considerable development. For example, the rear

Standing in the snow following its restoration by Dornier in 1975, this is the last surviving Do 335 and is part of the US National Air and Space Museum collection.

Dornier Do 335A-0

Weight: 9600kg (21,164lb)
Dimensions: Length 13.85m (45ft 5in), Wingspan 13.8m (45ft 3in), Height 5m (16ft 5in)
Powerplant: Two 1417kW (1900hp) Daimler-Benz DB 603E-1 inverted V-12 liquid-cooled piston engines
Speed: 763km/h (474mph)

Range: 1395km (867 miles)
Ceiling: 11,400m (37,400ft)
Crew: 1
Armament: One engine-mounted 30mm (1.18in) MK 103 cannon plus two 20mm (0.79in) MG 151/20 cannon; up to 1000kg (2200lb) in internal weapons bay

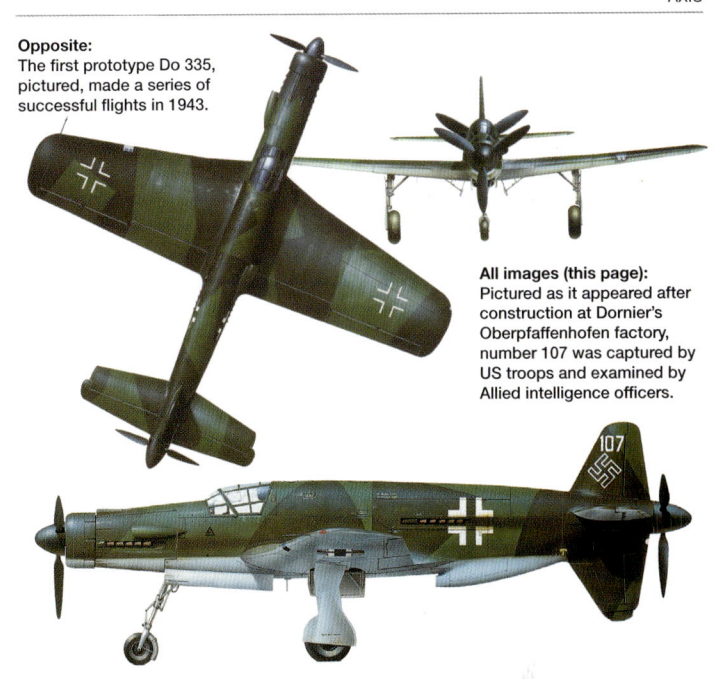

Opposite:
The first prototype Do 335, pictured, made a series of successful flights in 1943.

All images (this page):
Pictured as it appeared after construction at Dornier's Oberpfaffenhofen factory, number 107 was captured by US troops and examined by Allied intelligence officers.

engine drove its propeller by means of a drive shaft and this feature was tested on the small Göppingen Gö 9 research aircraft. Furthermore, the position of the propeller made the prospect of bailing out of the aircraft problematic for the pilot and as a result the Do 335 was one of the first aircraft to be fitted with an ejection seat.

Exceptional performance

The first Do 335 prototype made its maiden flight on 26 October 1943 and testing revealed that the aircraft possessed exceptional performance. The first 10 Do 335A-0 pre-production machines were used from May 1944 as reconnaissance aircraft but suffered teething issues, the most serious being a propensity for the rear engine to overheat. Nonetheless, fighter-bomber Do 335A-1s were being delivered by January 1945 but fewer than 15 had been built by the end of the war and their operational use, if any, is obscure.

Focke-Wulf Fw 190
(BMW 801-powered variants)

Often cited as the best all-round fighter aircraft produced in quantity in Germany during the war, the Focke-Wulf 190 broke new ground in radial-engined fighter design.

The Fw 190 boasted a much more tightly cowled radial engine than had been attempted before and relied on a powered fan just behind the propeller to supply enough air to the engine to cool it, a system that caused considerable trouble in development but which was ultimately solved. Eventually over 20,000 examples of the 'Butcher Bird' were produced, making it the second most produced

Ground attack was the major role of the Fw 190 in the last two years of war. These are Fw 190Fs of II Gruppe, Schlachtgeschwader 1 with bomb racks.

Focke-Wulf Fw 190A-8

Weight: 4900kg (10,800lb)
Dimensions: Length 8.95m (29ft 4in), Wingspan 10.50m (34ft 5in), Height 3.96m (13ft)
Powerplant: One 1567kW (2100hp) BMW 801D-2 14 cylinder air-cooled radial piston engine
Speed: 654km/h (408 mph)

Range: 805km (500 miles)
Ceiling: 11,400m (37,400ft)
Crew: 1
Armament: Two 7.92mm (0.31in) MG 17 machine guns, four 20mm (0.79in) MG 151/20 cannon; one 500kg (1100lb) and two 250kg (550lb) bombs

All images:
Based at Coquelles, near Calais, France, in November 1941, 6./JG 26 received some of the first production Fw 190A-1s. This example was flown by 20-victory ace Walter Schneider.

German aircraft after the Bf 109. Entering service in 1942, the Fw 190A initially proved superior to the contemporary Spitfire Mk.V on all counts except turn rate, prompting an intense British effort to match the German fighter.

Bomber interceptors

Focke-Wulf 190s were used to combat the daylight raids of the US 8th Air Force and heavily armoured variants were developed specifically to undertake the hazardous role of attacking heavy bombers. As the war progressed, the limitations of the BMW engine at altitude saw the Fw 190 increasingly used as a fighter-bomber where its excellent low-level performance was of great value. The Fw 190A-8 variant was the most produced subtype and could be used for both air superiority and ground attack missions but the various subtypes of the Fw190F and G were developed specifically for ground attack work.

Focke-Wulf Fw 190D and Ta 152

The substitution of the BMW 801 engine for the V-12 Jumo 213 was undertaken to improve the Fw 190's performance at altitude and resulted in an even more capable fighter.

The Fw 190D gained a longer nose due to the new inline engine and this required an extension to the rear fuselage, significantly altering the aircraft's profile. A liquid cooling system had to be fitted for the Jumo engine and this comprised an annular radiator, preserving the circular fuselage shape at the nose. In service from September 1944, the Fw 190D-9 proved the equal of any Allied fighter

The third prototype Ta 152C made its maiden flight in January 1945 and is seen here in wintery conditions during flight trials.

Focke-Wulf 190D-9

Weight: 4840kg (10,670lb)
Dimensions: Length 10.19m (33ft 5in), Wingspan 10.50m (34ft 5in), Height: 3.36m (11ft)
Powerplant: One 1320kW (1770hp) Junkers Jumo 213A-1 inverted V-12 liquid-cooled piston engine
Speed: 686km/h (426mph)

Range: 837km (520 miles)
Ceiling: 10,000m (32,800ft)
Crew: 1
Armament: Two 20mm (0.79in) MG 151/20 cannon, two 13mm (0.51in) MG 131 machine guns; provision for one 500kg (1100lb) SC 500 bomb

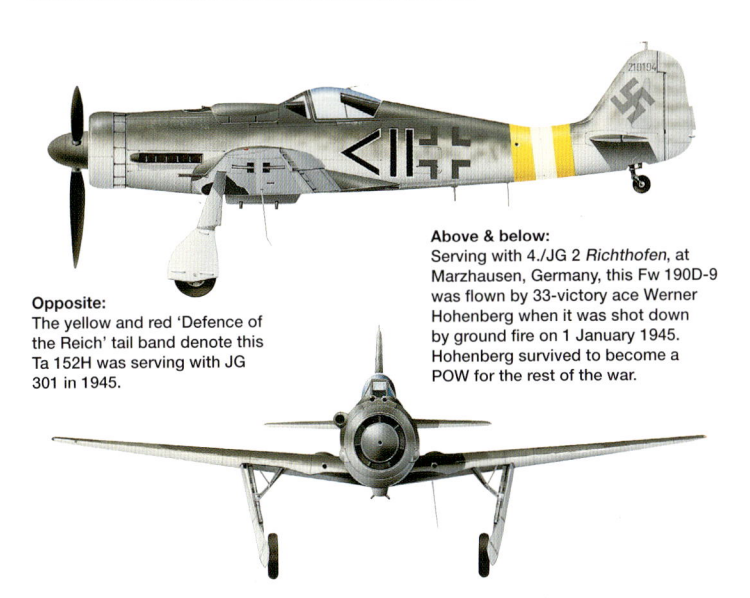

Above & below:
Serving with 4./JG 2 *Richthofen*, at Marzhausen, Germany, this Fw 190D-9 was flown by 33-victory ace Werner Hohenberg when it was shot down by ground fire on 1 January 1945. Hohenberg survived to become a POW for the rest of the war.

Opposite:
The yellow and red 'Defence of the Reich' tail band denote this Ta 152H was serving with JG 301 in 1945.

and possessed better dive and climb characteristics than the radial-engined Fw 190s, ideal for the dive-and-zoom tactics employed against the daylight bomber formations.

Manoeuvrable interceptor
The D-9 also boasted a better turn rate than its forebear, though it could not match the exceptional rate of roll of the earlier Fw 190s, and utilized the same wing as earlier models so its altitude performance, while better than the BMW-powered Fw 190, was not outstanding and it was always regarded as a stopgap until the appearance of the further developed Ta 152 (the 'Ta' designation reflecting the designer Kurt Tank). This introduced new wider chord tail surfaces, replaced the electrical flap and undercarriage operation with hydraulics and featured, in the Ta 152H, a high aspect ratio wing of colossal span optimized for high altitude flight. Fewer than 70 were built but their performance was excellent and the few examples that saw combat service in the closing days of the war proved formidable.

Heinkel He 162 *Volksjäger*

Developed at great speed, the He 162 was an attempt to produce a cheap, high-performance jet fighter to counter ever-increasing Allied daylight bombing raids.

The competition for a 'people's fighter' (*Volksjäger*) was initiated in September 1944 following major losses to the *Luftwaffe* fighter force. The aircraft was to be powered by a single BMW 003 turbojet engine, intended to be rapidly mass-produced using a minimum of strategic resources and flown by teenage pilots hastily trained on gliders. Heinkel's He 162 design was selected on

Seen here in British markings, this He 162 was tested in the UK but destroyed in a fatal crash on 7 September 1945 during a flying display.

Heinkel He 162A-1

Weight: 2800kg (6173lb)
Dimensions: Length 9.05m (29ft 8in), Wingspan 7.2m (23ft 7in), Height: 2.6m (8ft 6in)
Powerplant: One BMW-109-003E-1 Sturm axial flow jet engine, 800kg (1764lb) static thrust

Speed: 889km/h (553mph) at sea level (with emergency boosted thrust)
Range: 975km (606 miles)
Ceiling: 12,000m (39,000ft)
Crew: 1
Armament: Two 30mm (1.18in) MK 108 cannon

All images:
Karl-Emil Demuth assumed command of 3./JG 1 at Leck, Germany, on 5 May 1945. His aircraft, Yellow 11, has his score of 16 victories painted on the tail, though none of these were achieved with the He 162.

25 September and, amazingly, made its first flight less than 90 days later on 6 December. The aircraft was constructed largely of wood and utilized existing aircraft parts to speed development; the main undercarriage was the same as the Messerschmitt 109K, for example. The He 162 was designed to be largely disposable, damaged aircraft being discarded rather than repaired, but the pilot was provided with novel escape equipment in the form of an ejection seat. During its brief combat career, four ejections were attempted from *Volksjägers* but only two were successful.

Combat

Despite the loss of the prototype due to structural failure, the relentless pace of the programme resulted in initial deliveries being made to the first operational He 162 unit during February 1945. Although most of the rest of the war was spent in training, the He 162 did engage in some combat, scoring its first victory on 19 April over a Hawker Tempest.

Heinkel He 219 *Uhu*

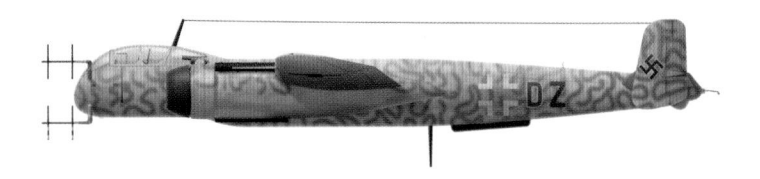

> **One of the best night fighters produced in Germany, the He 219 was not built in large numbers but nonetheless established an enviable combat record in the nocturnal skies of Germany.**

First flown on 6 November 1942, the He 219 *Uhu* ('Eagle Owl') had originally been schemed as a multi-purpose aircraft but would only ever serve operationally as a night fighter. A large and advanced aircraft, the He 219 was the world's first aircraft to feature ejection seats as standard and was also the first German design to enter service with a tricycle undercarriage. Initial operations in June 1943 were

Pictured on display in the US, this captured He 219 shows the considerable size of the 'antlers' of its Lichtenstein radar system.

Heinkel He 219A-2 *Uhu*

Weight: 15,300kg (33,730lb)
Dimensions: Length 15.55m (50ft 11in), Wingspan 18.5m (60ft 8in), Height 4.1m (13ft 5in)
Powerplant: Two 1305kW (1750hp) Daimler-Benz DB 603A inverted V-12 liquid-cooled piston engines
Speed: 665km/h (413mph)

Range: 1540km (957 miles)
Ceiling: 12,700m (41,666ft)
Crew: 2
Armament: Two 30mm (1.18in) MK 108 or MK 103 cannon, two 20mm (0.79in) MG1 51/20 cannon in ventral tray, and two MG 151/20s in the wing roots

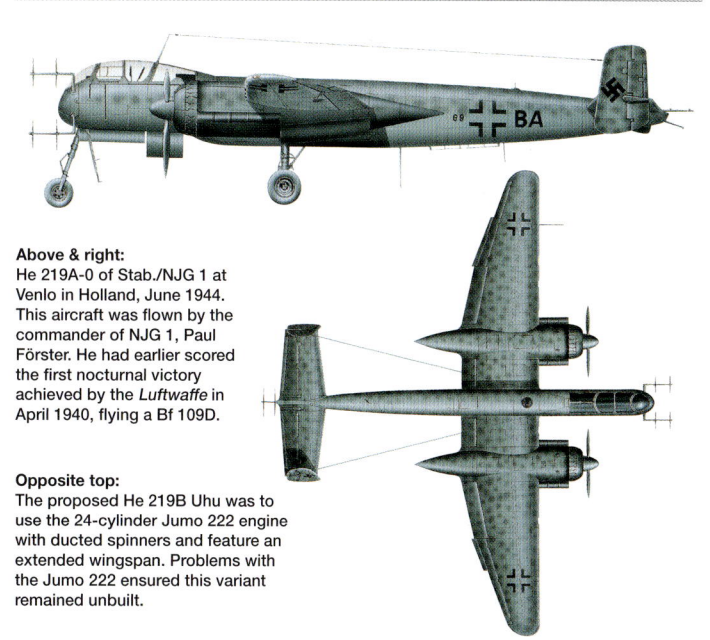

Above & right:
He 219A-0 of Stab./NJG 1 at Venlo in Holland, June 1944. This aircraft was flown by the commander of NJG 1, Paul Förster. He had earlier scored the first nocturnal victory achieved by the *Luftwaffe* in April 1940, flying a Bf 109D.

Opposite top:
The proposed He 219B Uhu was to use the 24-cylinder Jumo 222 engine with ducted spinners and feature an extended wingspan. Problems with the Jumo 222 ensured this variant remained unbuilt.

highly successful, with five British bombers destroyed in one sortie by the ninth prototype, out of a total of 20 claimed in the first six *Uhu* sorties. Despite this auspicious debut and the enthusiastic support of Josef Kammhuber, head of the night fighter force, the He 219 was cancelled by Erhard Milch, in charge of *Luftwaffe* procurement, due primarily to his personal dislike of Ernst Heinkel. Heinkel, however, simply ignored the cancellation and produced the He 219 anyway but in comparatively small numbers.

Heavy hitter

In service, the He 219 was prized by the crews who were lucky enough to fly it, with the aircraft receiving particular praise for its heavy armament. The ejection seats were credited with saving several crew members' lives and the He 219 was also easy to repair and service. The most successful *Uhu* pilot was Ernst-Wilhelm Modrow who shot down 33 bombers between March 1944 and January 1945.

Henschel Hs 123

Although apparently obsolete even in 1939, the biplane Hs 123 was an outstandingly effective close support aircraft and was used until the final few weeks of the war.

Ground attack was an area that had been profoundly neglected by most nations following World War I but experience in the Spanish Civil War showed that it was actually of crucial importance on the battlefield. The Hs 123 had been designed as a dive bomber but saw its usage change to a more general close support role during its service in Spain. Though only one squadron remained operational with

This Henschel Hs 123A-1 of *Schlachtgeschwader* 1 carries four SC 50 bombs under its wings.

Henschel Hs 123

Weight: 2217kg (4888lb)
Dimensions: Length 8.33m (27ft 4in), Wingspan 10.5m (34ft 5in), Height 3.2m (10ft 6in)
Powerplant: One 660kW (880hp) BMW 132Dc nine-cylinder air-cooled radial piston engine
Maximum speed: 341km/h (212mph)

Range: 860km (530 miles)
Ceiling: 9000m (30,000ft)
Crew: 1
Armament: Two 7.92mm (0.31in) MG 17 machine guns in upper forward fuselage; up to 450kg (992lb) of bombs under wings

Opposite:
This early Hs 123A was based at Fürstenfeldbruck, Bavaria, in October 1937 while serving with 7.Staffel of *Stukageschwader* 165 'Immelmann'.

Above & below:
Wearing the black triangle of the *Schlachtgeschwader* (literally translated as 'battle squadrons'), this winter-camouflaged Hs 123B of 5.(SchII)/LG 2, operating near Moscow in 1941, has lost its wheel spats as they tended to clog with mud.

the type at the outbreak of World War II, it subsequently saw service throughout the Polish campaign and across the low countries, proving highly effective and demonstrating the ability to fly more missions per day than any other unit.

Balkans campaign

Retired after the fall of France, the Hs 123 was subsequently returned to service for the Balkans campaign and went on to serve on the Eastern Front. The Hs 123 proved to be robust, durable and effective in combat, especially in severe conditions such as those pertaining in Russia that could not be tolerated by more advanced designs. So useful did it prove that as late as January 1943 *Generaloberst* Wolfram von Richthofen asked whether production of the Hs 123 could be restarted but by then the tooling had been scrapped. Surviving Hs 123s remained in the frontline until mid 1944.

Henschel Hs 129

A dedicated ground attack aircraft, the heavily armoured Hs 129 bridged the gap between tactical bombers and heavy fighters and proved effective against enemy armour.

Experience in Spain had demonstrated that there was a need for a dedicated close support aircraft and a specification was drawn up for a new combat type, the *Schlachtflugzeug* (literally 'battleplane'). The Hs 129 answered this requirement with the entire forward fuselage constructed of sheet steel, to protect the pilot, who was also given an amoured windscreen. The cockpit was

The 75mm (2.95in) 7,5 anti-tank gun fitted to the Hs 129B-3 was the heaviest weapon fitted to a production aircraft during the war.

Henschel Hs 129B-2

Weight: 5250kg (11,574lb)
Dimensions: Length 9.75m (32ft 0in), Wingspan 14.2m (46ft 7in), Height 3.25m (10ft 8in)
Powerplant: Two 515kW (691hp) Gnome-Rhône 14M-4/-5 14-cylinder air-cooled radial engines
Maximum speed: 407km/h (253mph)
Range: 690km (430 miles)

Ceiling: 9000m (30,000ft)
Crew: 1
Armament: Two 7.92mm (0.31in) MG 17 machine guns (later replaced with two 13mm (0.51in) MG 131 machine guns) and two 20mm MG 151/20 cannon; or one 30mm (1.18in) MK 101 cannon or MK 103 cannon in a conformally mounted gun pod

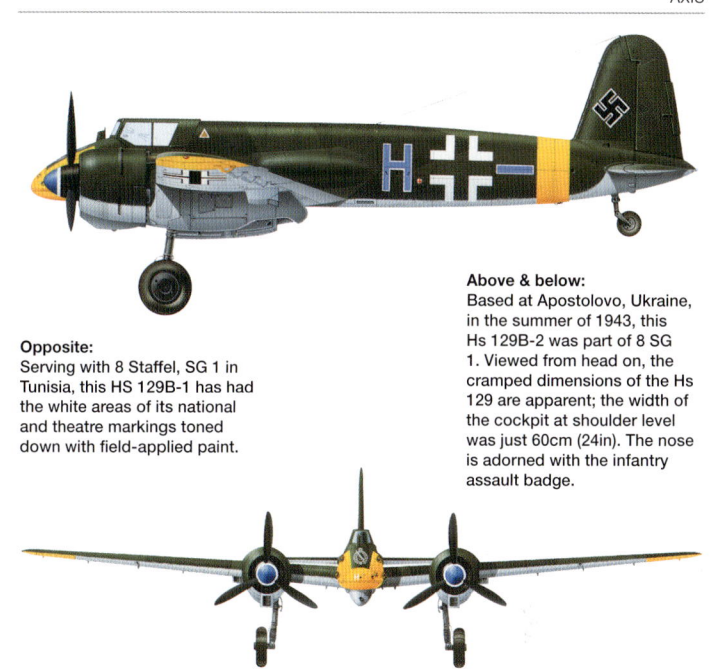

Opposite:
Serving with 8 Staffel, SG 1 in Tunisia, this HS 129B-1 has had the white areas of its national and theatre markings toned down with field-applied paint.

Above & below:
Based at Apostolovo, Ukraine, in the summer of 1943, this Hs 129B-2 was part of 8 SG 1. Viewed from head on, the cramped dimensions of the Hs 129 are apparent; the width of the cockpit at shoulder level was just 60cm (24in). The nose is adorned with the infantry assault badge.

cramped, requiring the gunsight to be fitted externally, and some engine instruments were mounted in the nacelles. Powered by air-cooled Argus V8 engines, the Hs 129A-1 proved woefully underpowered and was rejected by the *Luftwaffe*. French Gnome-Rhône 14M radial engines were substituted and in this form the Hs 129 entered production and service.

Eastern Front service

Initial use was in Tunisia but the aircraft saw the majority of its service on the Eastern Front where the aircraft was much in demand for the anti-tank role. Improvements to Soviet armour saw the Hs 129 progressively up-gunned until it mounted a 7.5cm (2.95in) semi-automatic Rheinmetall PaK 40 anti-tank gun, the most powerful forward-firing weapon fitted to any production aircraft during World War II, and theoretically capable of penetrating any tank in the world.

Junkers Ju 88

> The Ju 88 was a medium bomber that possessed sufficient performance for it to be used as a successful heavy fighter, becoming the *Luftwaffe*'s most numerous night fighter.

The high performance of the Ju 88 bomber had spurred interest in its use as a fighter even before the war and the first of a purpose-designed *Zerstörer* variant appeared in mid 1938 as the Ju 88C. The initial production Ju 88C-2 was built only in small numbers and used for intruder missions over the UK as well as anti-shipping work. Further development resulted in the more heavily armed Ju

This Ju 88G-6 I is equipped with radar for the night-fighter role.

Junkers Ju 88G-7a

Weight: 13,109kg (28,900lb)
Dimensions: Length 14.5m (47ft 6 in), Wingspan 22m (72ft 2in), Height 5.07m (16ft 7in)
Powerplant: Two 1287kW (1726hp) Junkers Jumo 213E inverted V-12 liquid-cooled piston engines
Speed: 647km/h (402mph)

Range: 2200km (1367 miles)
Ceiling: 9800m (32,100ft)
Crew: 4
Armament: Six 20mm (0.79in) MG 151/20 cannon (two in the nose and four in a ventral tray), one defensive 13mm (0.51in) MG 131 machine gun flexibly mounted in rear cockpit

Opposite:
Night-fighter crews went to considerable lengths to reduce the visibility of their aircraft. This Ju 88 of NG 2 has had all markings virtually obliterated to render it less conspicuous.

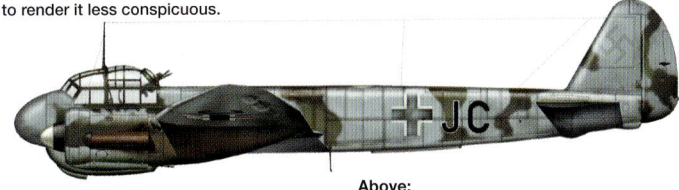

Above:
Ju 88C-6 of V./KG 40, 1943. Operating as heavy fighters over the Bay of Biscay, Ju 88s made operations hazardous for Allied aircraft flying in the area and prompted the use of long-range Mosquitos to counter the threat.

Below:
Based at Ingolstadt, Bavaria, this Ju 88G-6b of I./NJG 101 is fitted with a *Schräge musik* installation and features a replacement rudder.

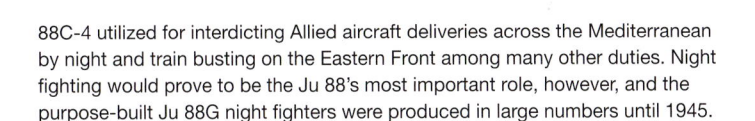

88C-4 utilized for interdicting Allied aircraft deliveries across the Mediterranean by night and train busting on the Eastern Front among many other duties. Night fighting would prove to be the Ju 88's most important role, however, and the purpose-built Ju 88G night fighters were produced in large numbers until 1945.

Night fighter

Night-fighting Ju 88s were often fitted with the upward firing *Schräge musik* installation and standardly carried *Lichtenstein* radar, initially in B/C form with the dense 'mattress' aerial array then later the SN-2 set with its large 'stag's antlers' aerials. Flensburg FuG 227 gear also homed in on the 'Monica' tail warning radars of RAF bombers. Later, *Naxos* was developed that detected H2S radar that homed in on H2S radar and the last few Ju 88G-7s featured Berlin N-1a (FuG 340) centimetric radar, based on captured cavity magnetron technology. The Ju 88 proved highly successful against RAF heavy bombers by night but was itself vulnerable to higher-performance Mosquito night fighters.

Messerschmitt Bf 109A–E

Germany's most important single-seater, and the most produced fighter design in history, the Bf 109 saw action in Spain before outclassing every fighter in its path during the early war years.

Initially produced by BFW, of which Willy Messerschmitt was the chief designer, the Bf 109 beat the rival Heinkel He 112 to become Germany's first high-performance, stressed skin, cantilever monoplane fighter. Somewhat ironically, given what was to come, the first prototype was powered by a British Rolls-Royce Kestrel engine and made its maiden flight on 29 May 1935, with the first

Leutnant Steindl, the Geschwader adjutant of JG 54, positions his Bf 109E-4B for a wingman's camera during a bombing mission to Stalingrad in spring 1942.

Messerschmitt Bf 109E-4

Weight: 2505kg (5523lb)
Dimensions: Length 8.76m (28ft 7in), Wingspan 9.87m (32ft 4in), Height 2.2m (7ft 5in)
Powerplant: One 894kW (1200hp) Daimler-Benz DB601N liquid-cooled inverted-V-12 piston engine

Speed: 570km/h (354mph)
Range: 700km (435 miles)
Ceiling: 10,500m (34,450ft)
Crew: 1
Armament: Two 20mm (0.79in) MG FF/M wing cannon, two 7.92mm (0.31in) MG 17 machine guns

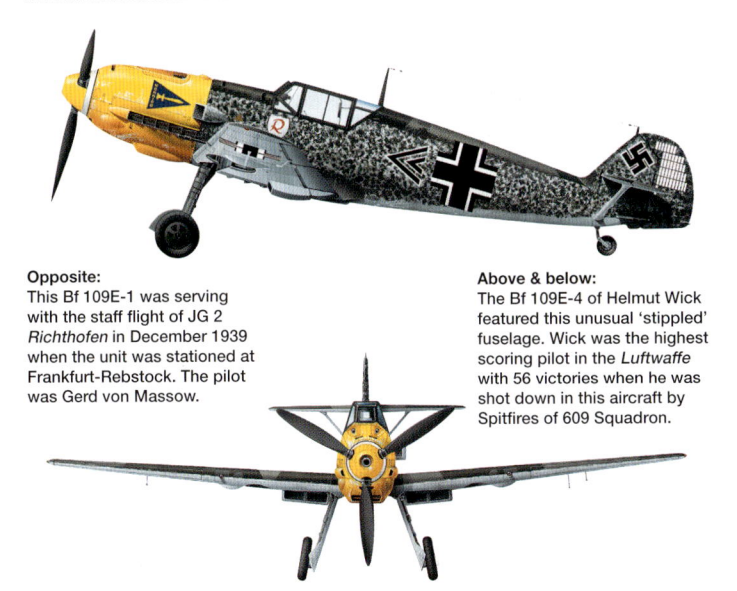

Opposite:
This Bf 109E-1 was serving with the staff flight of JG 2 *Richthofen* in December 1939 when the unit was stationed at Frankfurt-Rebstock. The pilot was Gerd von Massow.

Above & below:
The Bf 109E-4 of Helmut Wick featured this unusual 'stippled' fuselage. Wick was the highest scoring pilot in the *Luftwaffe* with 56 victories when he was shot down in this aircraft by Spitfires of 609 Squadron.

example with a German engine, initially the Junkers Jumo 210, flying later that year. Only 22 Bf 109As were built before production switched to the more powerful Bf 109B and minor changes resulted in the Bf 109C and D. Some of these early Jumo-powered Bf 109s were used in Spain where they performed well, if not spectacularly.

The major change to the aircraft occurred in 1938 when the Daimler-Benz 601 engine replaced the Jumo, resulting in a leap in performance. A few Bf 109Es fought in Spain, utterly outclassing all other fighters, before the aircraft spearheaded the *Blitzkrieg* campaigns in Poland, the Low Countries and France, sweeping aside virtually all fighter opposition. The Bf 109E finally met its match in the Spitfire during the Battle of Britain, with the two aircraft proving remarkably evenly matched. After the Bf 109F took over the air superiority role, later Bf 109Es operated as fighter-bombers with *Schlacht* units into 1943 and many were exported to friendly nations, resulting in the bizarre situation of the aircraft fighting itself when Yugoslavian Bf 109Es clashed with Luftwaffe Bf 109Es during the German invasion of April 1941.

Messerschmitt Bf 109F–K

Following a redesign of the Bf 109's airframe, mass production really got into its stride and vast swarms of Bf 109G variants swarmed the skies from 1942 onwards.

The Bf 109F introduced a more streamlined fuselage and new rounded wingtips as well as dispensing with the tail struts of the Bf 109E. Widely considered the best handling of the 109 series, it became the primary fighter spearheading the invasion of the Soviet Union as well as seeing considerable action in the Western Desert. A switch to the more powerful but heavier DB 605 engine resulted in

Bf 109G-6s of 7./JG 27 patrol over the Adriatic from their base in Greece.

Messerschmitt Bf 109G-10

Weight: 3400kg (7496lb)
Dimensions: Length 8.95m (29ft4in), Wingspan 9.9m (32ft 7in), Height 2.6m (8ft 6in)
Powerplant: One 1250kW (1677hp) DB 605D-2 inverted V-12 liquid-cooled piston engine

Speed: 640km/h (400mph)
Range: 850km (530 miles)
Ceiling: 12,000m (39,000ft)
Crew: 1
Armament: Two 20mm (0.8in) MG 151/2 cannon, two 13mm (0.51in) MG 131 machine guns

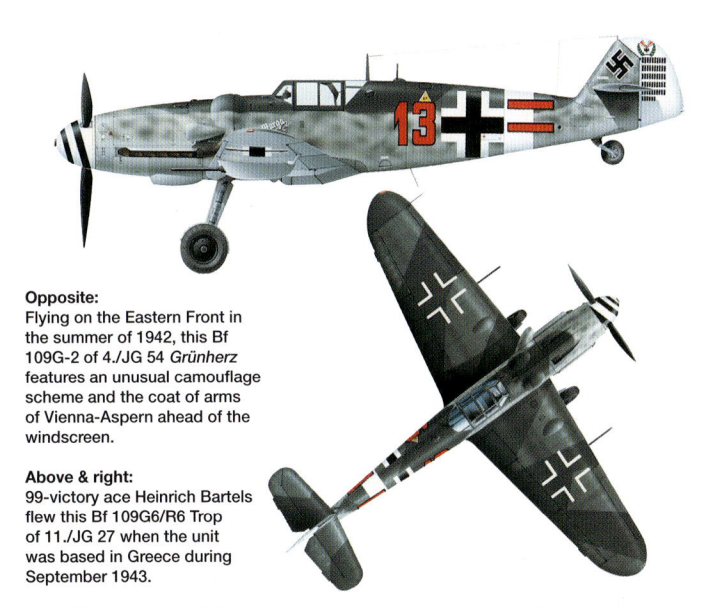

Opposite:
Flying on the Eastern Front in the summer of 1942, this Bf 109G-2 of 4./JG 54 *Grünherz* features an unusual camouflage scheme and the coat of arms of Vienna-Aspern ahead of the windscreen.

Above & right:
99-victory ace Heinrich Bartels flew this Bf 109G6/R6 Trop of 11./JG 27 when the unit was based in Greece during September 1943.

the 109G which would become the most produced variant, though increasing weight due to upgrading armament and equipment eroded the flying qualities of the type and manoeuvrability and handling both suffered. The Bf 109G was built in a bewildering number of subtypes for a variety of missions with fighter-bomber, reconnaissance, high-altitude and lightened versions all appearing.

Bf 109K

To further complicate matters, *Rüstsätze* field kits were supplied to modify aircraft to specific roles at unit level. A late-war attempt to rationalize production aircraft led to the Bf 109K which was intended to be offered in three basic versions, though in the event these were all abandoned and mass production was further rationalized in the form of a fourth, the Bf 109K-4.

Following the end of hostilities, Spain built a 109 variant powered by a Rolls-Royce Merlin and in Czechoslovakia the Avia S.199 was produced powered by the Jumo 211, which ironically would see this iconic Nazi-era design form the nascent fighter force of Israel.

Messerschmitt Bf 110A–F

The *Zerstörer* ('destroyer') concept of a long-range, heavily armed, twin-engined fighter was embodied in the Bf 110, expected to offset any deficiency in manoeuvrability with firepower and speed.

Intended to operate primarily as a heavy fighter but with a secondary fighter-bomber capability, the Bf 110 flew for the first time on 12 May 1936. Persistent engine problems afflicted initial aircraft and the first serially produced aircraft were the Bf 110B-1, powered by the Jumo 210. The engine was soon switched to the powerful DB 601 resulting in the Bf 110C and the long-range Bf 110D derivative with

A Bf 110C-4b, fitted with a ventral bomb rack, during the North African campaign, 1942.

Messerschmitt Bf 110E-1

Weight: 6750kg (14,881lb)
Dimensions: Length 12.1m (39ft 8in), Wingspan 16.2m (53ft 2in), Height 3.5m (11ft 6in)
Powerplant: Two 895kW (1200hp) Daimler-Benz DB 601N-1 inverted V-12 liquid-cooled piston engines
Speed: 560km/h (349mph)

Range: 775km (482 miles)
Ceiling: 8000m (26,245ft)
Crew: 2
Armament: Two 20mm (0.79in) MG FF/M cannon and four 7.92mm (0.31in) MG 17 machine guns fixed in nose, one 7.92mm (0.31in) MG 15 machine gun in rear cockpit; four ETC 50 bomb racks for bombload 1200kg (2645lb)

Opposite:
Brand-new Bf 110C still in the factory codes applied for
flight testing. Unit markings will replace these letters
when the aircraft is assigned to an operational unit.

Above:
This Bf 110C was assigned to
the staff flight of 1./JG 2. Bf 110s
were popular for headquarters
duties due to their ability to carry
up to two passengers or perform
reconnaissance.

Below:
Serving with 8./ZG 26 in Libya
in late 1941, this Bf 110E
features the standard tropical
Luftwaffe finish of RLM 79
Sandgelb (sand yellow) over
RLM 78 *Himmelblau* (sky blue).

further engine improvements resulting in the Bf 110E and long-range F. The Bf
110 first saw action during the invasion of Poland, proving a great success in
that campaign while recording impressive results as a bomber interceptor, on
one occasion shooting down 22 Wellington bombers of the RAF during a single
raid in December 1939.

Zerstörer concept

However, the limitations of the *Zerstörer* concept were made brutally apparent
when the Bf 110 was committed to the Battle of Britain and found itself unable
to deal with modern single-seaters. Lacking the manoeuvrability to effectively
combat such aircraft and possessing inadequate defensive armament to protect
itself, losses were heavy. Combat use of the Bf 110 was modified following this
experience and the type continued to serve successfully, acting as a potent
fighter-bomber in North Africa and on the Eastern Front and finding its niche in
Western Europe as an effective night fighter.

Messerschmitt Bf 110G

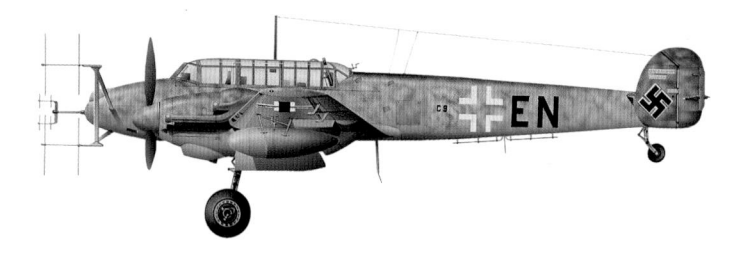

Produced in the wake of the Me 210 debacle, the Bf 110G was the last variant to be produced in large numbers including the definitive Bf 110G-4 night fighter.

The failure of the Me 210 programme left the *Luftwaffe* with a gap in its inventory and the decision was taken to further develop the Bf 110, resulting in the DB 605-powered Bf 110G. The new variant could be easily identified by its use of the more streamlined engine nacelles of the Me 210 and serial production began in December 1942 after an initial batch of G-0 pre-series aircraft had been produced.

The Lichtenstein BC radar improved the chances of a Bf 110 finding a bomber at night, but it cut 40km/h (25mph) from the top speed.

Messerschmitt Bf 110G-4b/R3

Weight: 6750kg (14,881lb)
Dimensions: Length 13.05m (42ft 8in), Wingspan 16.27m (53ft 4in), Height 3.5m (11ft 6in)
Powerplant: Two 1100kW (1475hp) DB 605B inverted V-12 liquid-cooled piston engines
Speed: 560km/h (349mph)
Range: 775km (482 miles)

Ceiling: 10,900m (35,760ft)
Crew: 2 or 3
Armament: Two 30mm (1.18in) MK 108 and two 20mm (0.79in) MG 151/20 cannons firing forward in nose and optional fitting of two MG 151/20 or two MK 108 cannons firing obliquely upwards in rear cockpit; optional ventral tray with two MG 151/20 firing forward

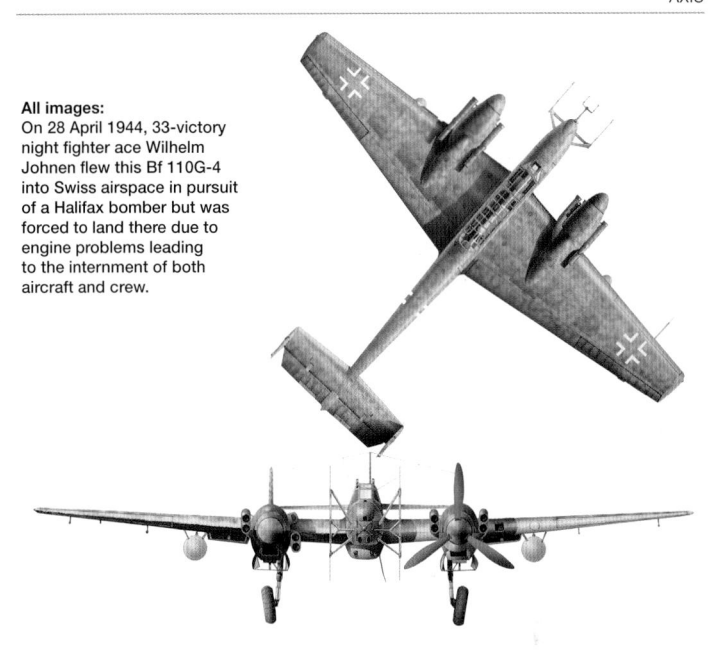

All images:
On 28 April 1944, 33-victory night fighter ace Wilhelm Johnen flew this Bf 110G-4 into Swiss airspace in pursuit of a Halifax bomber but was forced to land there due to engine problems leading to the internment of both aircraft and crew.

Reflecting operational reality, which had demonstrated the vulnerability of the Bf 110 in air combat by day, no examples of the heavy fighter G-1 variant were built, the G-2 fighter-bomber becoming the first production subtype to appear. The G-3 was a reconnaissance variant but the G-4 night fighter would prove the most important of the G series.

New radar sets

Messerschmitt had produced a dedicated, radar-equipped Bf 110 with the F-4 series in 1942 and the G-4 initially sported the same FuG 202 *Lichtenstein* radar, and introduced optional *Schräge Musik* upward firing cannon. The aircraft subsequently incorporated ever-improving radar sets as they became available and formed the backbone of the *Luftwaffe* night fighter forces in 1943–44, proving highly successful, though losses were sometimes severe. The most successful night fighter pilot in history, Heinz-Wolfgang Schnaufer, used the Bf 110 to shoot down 121 RAF bombers between June 1942 and March 1945.

Messerschmitt Me 210

Planned as an advanced successor to the Bf 110, the Me 210 was crippled by severe problems and the programme proved a costly failure for the *Luftwaffe*.

When the *Luftwaffe* requested a replacement *Zerstörer*, Messerschmitt submitted the Me 210 design in competition with the Arado Ar 240. On paper, the Me 210 was an excellent prospect, featuring a shorter nose than the Bf 110 for better visibility, a weapons bay under the cockpit meaning that speed wasn't compromised by drag-inducing ordnance mounted externally, and

Early production Me 210A-1 in flight in 1942. The Me 210 was aesthetically striking and featured heavily in German propaganda.

Messerschmitt Me 210A-1

Weight: 9705kg (21,396lb)
Dimensions: Length 12.2m (40ft), Wingspan 16.3m (53ft 6in), Height 4.2m (13ft 9in)
Powerplant: Two 990kW (1330hp) Daimler-Benz DB 601F inverted V-12 liquid-cooled piston engines
Speed: 463km/h (288mph)
Range: 1818km (1130 miles)

Ceiling: 8900m (29,200ft)
Crew: 2
Armament: Two 20mm (0.79in) MG 151/20 cannon, two 7.92mm (0.31in) MG 17 machine guns, two remotely controlled rear-firing 13mm (0.51in) MG 131 machine guns; up to 1000kg (2200b) bombload in internal weapons bay

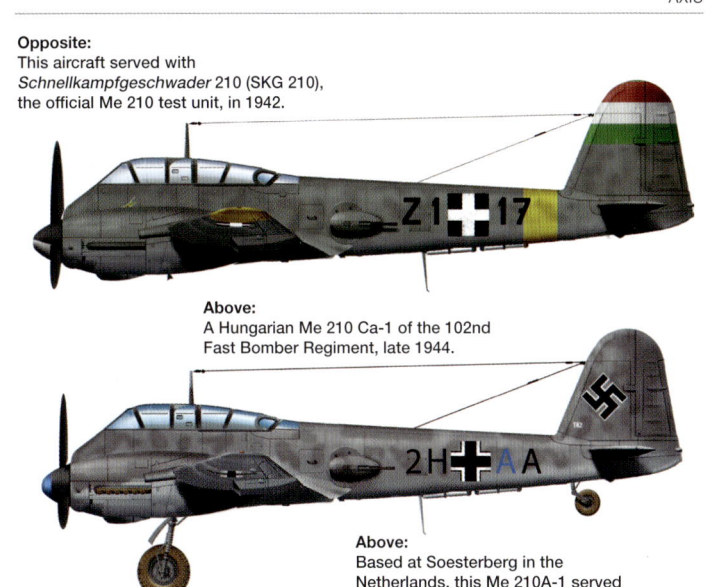

Opposite:
This aircraft served with
Schnellkampfgeschwader 210 (SKG 210),
the official Me 210 test unit, in 1942.

Above:
A Hungarian Me 210 Ca-1 of the 102nd
Fast Bomber Regiment, late 1944.

Above:
Based at Soesterberg in the
Netherlands, this Me 210A-1 served
with *Erprobungsstaffel* 210 in 1942.

a remote-controlled rear gun system that gave a much improved field of fire
than the manually aimed gun of the Bf 110. The cleaned up aerodynamics
promised a high top speed and, with Messerschmitt's reputation riding high on
the success of the Bf 109 and 110, 1000 examples of the Me 210 were ordered
'off the drawing board' before the prototype had even flown. This proved to be
a dreadful mistake, flight testing revealed appalling handling issues prompting
Messerschmitt's chief test pilot to comment that the Me 210 had 'all the least
desirable attributes an aeroplane could possess'.

Brief service

Unstable, underpowered and prone to violent and unheralded stalls, an
unprecedented 16 prototypes and 94 pre-production examples were built to try
to resolve the problems. Notwithstanding its unacceptable handling, deliveries
to operational units began in May 1942, where the Me 210, unsurprisingly,
proved unpopular and all were retired after brief service with further Bf 110
production taking place instead.

Messerschmitt Me 410 *Hornisse*

The Me 210 was further developed into the Me 410, finally evolving into an acceptable combat aircraft following major changes to its wing and fuselage.

A curious aspect of the Me 210 story was that it was produced under licence by the Danubian Aircraft Plant in Hungary but these aircraft featured more powerful DB 605 engines and a lengthened fuselage, the latter a design change recommended by the test pilot after the Me 210's first flight but rejected on the grounds of cost. Hungarian Me 210Cs proved generally acceptable in service and

The remote control barbette on the fuselage side is obvious here. Although technically complicated it provided excellent rear defence.

Messerschmitt Me 410A-1

Weight: 9651kg (21,276lb)
Dimensions: Length 12.4m (40ft 11.5in), Wingspan 16.3m (53ft 8in), Height 4.3m (14ft)
Powerplant: Two 1300kW (1750hp) Daimler-Benz DB 603A inverted V-12 liquid-cooled piston engines
Speed: 624km/h (388mph)
Range: 1690km (1050 miles)

Ceiling: 10,000m (33,000ft)
Crew: 2
Armament: Two 20mm (0.79in) MG 151/20 cannon, two 7.92mm (0.31in) MG 17 machine guns, two remotely controlled rear-firing 13mm (0.51in) MG 131 machine guns; up to 1000kg (2200b) bombload in internal weapons bay

Opposite top:
The Me 410A-1/U4 was the most spectacular subvariant as it was fitted with a 50mm (2in) Bordkanone BK-5 cannon with 22 rounds and intended for destroying bombers.

Above:
Me 410 of 9./ZG 1. The heavily armed Me 410 initially achieved considerable success against unescorted day-flying US bombers but lacked the performance and manoeuvrability to deal with escort fighters.

Messerschmitt in Germany subsequently fitted even more powerful DB 603 engines, belatedly lengthened the fuselage and redesigned the wing, thus curing the worst of the Me 210's foibles. In this form, dubbed Me 410 to imply it was a new design, the aircraft began to be delivered in early 1943.

Fighter-bomber role

In service the Me 410 was fast and impressively armed and was successful in bringing down many USAAF bombers but struggled when faced with escort fighters, lacking the manoeuvrability to deal with such types as the P-51 Mustang. Although it proved to be an excellent fighter-bomber, making numerous attacks against targets in the heavily defended south of England, it was decided that the Me 410 did not offer a sufficient increase in performance over the older and less expensive Bf 110 and production was terminated after 1160 examples had been built.

Messerschmitt Me 163 *Komet*

The most radical aircraft fielded by any of the combatants in World War II, the astonishingly fast *Komet* remains the only rocket-powered aircraft to have entered service.

Aerodynamicist Alexander Lippisch had been working on tailless designs since before the war and was in the process of adapting such a design for rocket propulsion when he and his design team were transferred to the Messerschmitt company. Three prototypes were constructed, the first powered flight occurring on 1 September 1941 and in October one of the prototypes became the

An Me 163B-1a launching at Bad Zwischenahn, home of Erprobungskommando 16, which accepted its first Me 163B during May 1944.

Messerschmitt Me 163B-1 *Komet*

Weight: 4310kg (9500lb)
Dimensions: Length 5.85m (19ft 2in), Wingspan 9.4m (30ft 7in), Height 2.76m (9ft)
Powerplant: One Walter HWK 109-509A rocket motor delivering 14.71kN (3307lb) of thrust

Speed: 955km/h (593mph)
Range: 35.5km (22 miles)
Ceiling: 12,000m (39,370ft)
Crew: 1
Armament: Two 30mm (1.18in) MK 108 cannon in wings

Opposite:
The first operational Me 163 mission was flown by Wolfgang Späte in this all-red *Komet*.

Above:
A development airframe of *Erprobungskommando* 16, V35 was painted in all-over light grey, apart from the rudder in a darker hue.

Below:
Operational Me 163 of JG 400, the only unit to fly the Me 163 in combat. JG 400 was based at Brandis, near Leipzig, Germany.

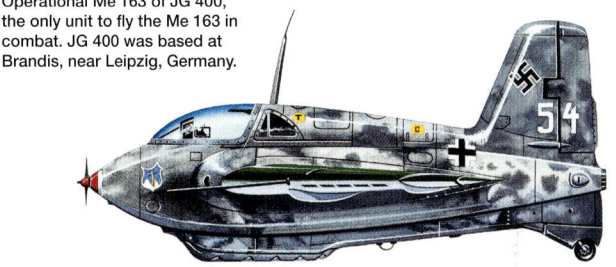

first aircraft to exceed 1000km/h (620mph) in level flight, around 250km/h (124mph) faster than the world absolute airspeed record. Plans were set in train to produce the aircraft as a point defence interceptor resulting in the operational Me 163B which, with its ability to climb 12,000m (39,000ft) in three minutes, could attack bombing raids at very short notice.

The first combat sortie was flown in May 1944 and the Me 163 was operational until early May 1945. However, despite its incredible performance and docile handling, the *Komet* was a flawed and dangerous aircraft: its endurance was measured in minutes and it had to glide back to base, once landed it couldn't taxi and was vulnerable to attack, its enormous speed made accurate aiming at much slower moving aircraft difficult but worst of all its volatile and corrosive fuels exploded if they came into contact with each other, as could, and did, happen in a rough landing. Ultimately only nine Allied aircraft were confirmed shot down by *Komets*.

Messerschmitt Me 262

A truly epoch-making aircraft, the Me 262 was the first jet fighter both to enter service and engage in combat, and ushered in a new age of combat aircraft.

The Me 262 project began before the war but the slow progress of jet engine development meant that the aircraft would not make a flight on jet power alone until July 1942. Initially fitted with a conventional tailwheel undercarriage, a tricycle arrangement was soon adopted on later prototypes and after much development work the first batch of Me 262A-1a fighters began to be delivered to the *Luftwaffe*

This Messerschmitt Me 262A-2 was one of 350 A-2a fighter bombers supplied to KG 51 from September 1944 onwards.

Messerschmitt Me 262A-1a

Weight: 6775kg (14,936lb)
Dimensions: Length 10.61m (34ft 9.5in), Wingspan 12.50m (41ft 0in), Height: 3.83m (12ft 7in)
Powerplant: Two 8.8kN (1890lb) Junkers Jumo 004B-1 turbojets

Speed: 870km/h (541mph)
Range: 845km (525 miles)
Ceiling: 11,000m (36,090ft)
Crew: 1
Armament: Four 30mm (1.18in) MK 108A-3 cannon in nose

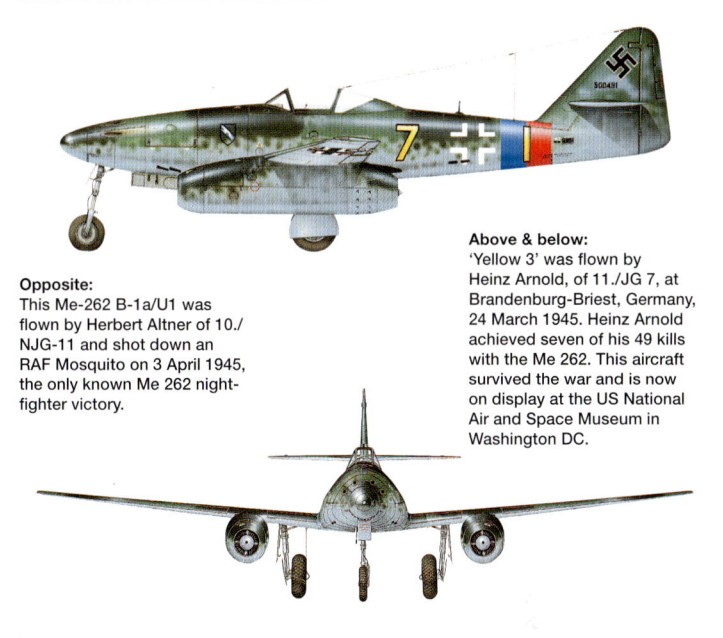

Opposite:
This Me-262 B-1a/U1 was flown by Herbert Altner of 10./NJG-11 and shot down an RAF Mosquito on 3 April 1945, the only known Me 262 night-fighter victory.

Above & below:
'Yellow 3' was flown by Heinz Arnold, of 11./JG 7, at Brandenburg-Briest, Germany, 24 March 1945. Heinz Arnold achieved seven of his 49 kills with the Me 262. This aircraft survived the war and is now on display at the US National Air and Space Museum in Washington DC.

in July 1944. The first air-to-air victory by a jet aircraft took place on 8 August 1944 when Lt. Joachim Weber shot down a reconnaissance Mosquito over Munich. The main mission for the Me 262, however, was to intercept daylight bombing raids and the aircraft proved effective in this role, though its usefulness was somewhat diminished by its vulnerability when landing and taking off: both operations requiring a long, straight and slow flight to or from the airfield.

Unreliable engines
The Me 262 was also hampered by its unreliable engines, compromised by the limited availability of high-quality steel. However, the jets ran on diesel or J2 fuel, derived from brown coal, and suffered less acutely from fuel shortages than the piston-engined types which required scarce high-octane supplies. Me 262s were also utilized as fighter bombers, famously attacking the bridge at Remagen, and as effective reconnaissance aircraft, their speed rendering them largely immune from interception.

Fiat CR.32 *Freccia*

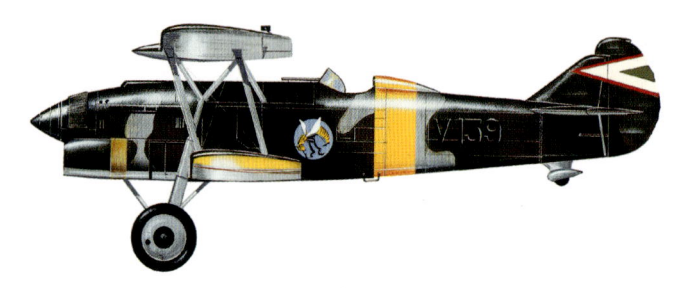

One of the most successful aircraft of the Spanish Civil War, the CR.32 was obsolete at the outbreak of World War II but nonetheless saw considerable active service.

The CR.32 was one of the finest fighters in the world when it appeared in 1933 and was used to great effect in Spain where its considerable success against the more advanced monoplane Polikarpov I-16 became one of the main reasons that the Italian high command believed there was still a place for agile biplane fighters in a modern air force. By the time Italy entered World War II in June 1940, the

This Cr.32bis was captured intact by Republican forces in Spain and photographed at Los Alcanzares airfield during testing.

Fiat CR.32

Weight: 1975kg (4354lb)
Dimensions: Length 7.47m (24ft 6in), Wingspan 9.5m (31ft 2in), Height 2.36m (7ft 9in)
Powerplant: One 447kW (599hp) Fiat A.30 R.A.bis liquid-cooled V-12 piston engine
Maximum speed: 360km/h (220mph)

Range: 781km (485 miles)
Ceiling: 8,800m (28,900ft)
Crew: 1
Armament: 7.7mm (0.303in) or 12.7mm (0.5in) Breda-SAFAT machine guns; up to 100kg (220lb) bombload

Opposite:
1./1 Squadron of the Hungarian 1st Fighter Group operated this CR.32 at Börgönd airfield, east of Lake Balaton, Hungary.

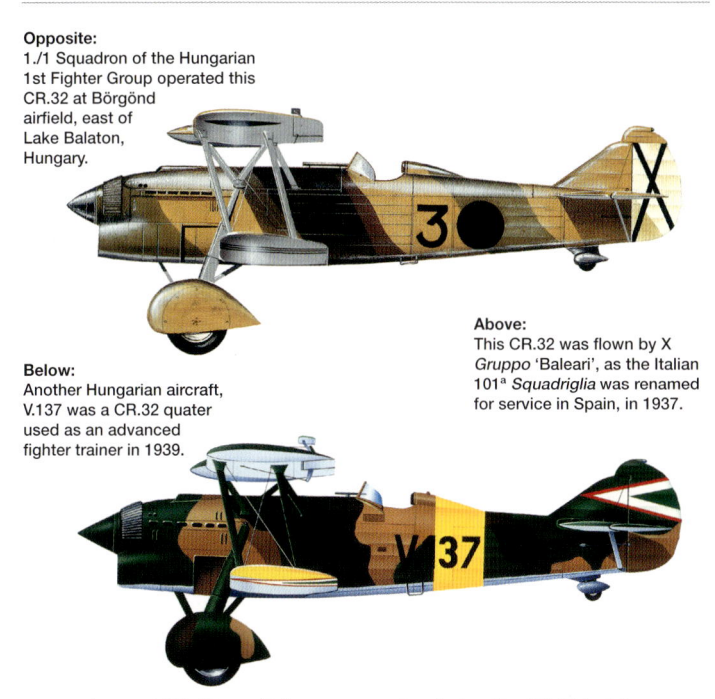

Above:
This CR.32 was flown by X *Gruppo* 'Baleari', as the Italian 101ª *Squadriglia* was renamed for service in Spain, in 1937.

Below:
Another Hungarian aircraft, V.137 was a CR.32 quater used as an advanced fighter trainer in 1939.

more advanced CR.42 was in the process of replacing the CR.32 but there were still large numbers of the older aircraft in service.

East African campaign

During the East African campaign of mid 1940 the CR.32s repeatedly managed to score victories against more advanced aircraft, such as the Hawker Hurricane, although supply difficulties saw the CR.32 inventory dwindle until only one was left in that theatre by April 1941. CR.32s were also utilized in the invasion of Greece but by 1942 the type was restricted to training and night fighting in the *Regia Aeronautica*. Hungary also used the CR.32, establishing air superiority over Slovakia in the brief war of early 1939 before operating two squadrons against the Soviet Union during the opening of Operation Barbarossa in July 1941. These, however, were soon relegated to training.

Fiat CR.42 *Falco*

The final fighter biplane to be developed in Italy, the CR.42 became the most produced Italian aircraft of the war and served with several export nations.

The CR.42 flew for the first time in May 1938. Too late to see service in the Spanish Civil War, it would fire its guns in anger for the first time in Belgian hands, scoring five confirmed victories against invading German aircraft, two of which were Messerschmitt Bf 109s. Italian use of the *Falco* ('Falcon') in combat began in the late stages of the Battle for France though the aircraft is perhaps best known for its service

The overall silver CR.42 prototype bore no markings save for national markings and constructor's number as it had been developed as a private venture by Fiat.

Fiat CR.42 *Falco*

Weight: 2295kg (5060lb)
Dimensions: Length 8.25m (27ft 1in), Wingspan 9.7m (31ft 10in), Height 3.59m (11ft 9in)
Powerplant: One 627kW (841hp) Fiat A.74 R1 C.38 14-cylinder air-cooled radial piston engine
Speed: 441km/h (274mph)

Range: 780km (480 miles)
Ceiling: 10,210m (33,500ft)
Crew: 1
Armament: Two 12.7mm (0.5in) Breda-SAFAT machine guns; two 100kg (220lb) bombs on underwing racks

Opposite:
Sweden designated its CR.42 the J 11. This *Fllygflottilj* 9 example was based at Säve, near Gothenburg, Sweden, in late 1942.

Above:
Hungary took delivery of 52 examples of the Fiat biplane. V-252 was based at Budapest in 1941 and flew with the 1st Fighter Regiment.

Above:
The Hungarian Air Force flew their CR.42s over the Eastern Front as part of Operation 'Barbarossa'. Wearing the markings adopted in 1942, V.232 was operating with the Hungarian Fast Corps.

in East Africa where it regularly clashed with RAF Gloster Gladiators. The two aircraft were well matched but in this campaign the *Falco* established superiority over the British biplane: on one occasion in November 1940, for example, CR.42s tangled with Gladiators and destroyed seven for no loss.

Greek campaign

The CR.42 was Italy's main fighter type during the Greek campaign but it was subsequently replaced by more modern monoplane fighters, engaging in a secondary career as a highly accurate close-support aircraft for the rest of the war, a role in which it was also utilized by the *Luftwaffe*. Hungary was also a major *Falco* operator, flying the CR.42 in combat on the Eastern Front until the end of 1941.

Fiat G.50 *Freccia*

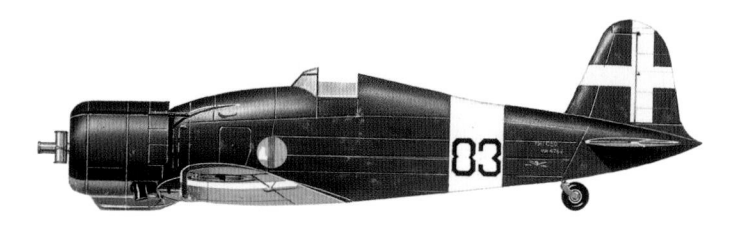

The first cantilever monoplane fighter adopted by Italy was a workmanlike if unspectacular combat aircraft, though it proved remarkably successful in Finland.

Fiat's first cantilever monoplane fighter, the G.50 *Freccia* ('Arrow') flew for the first time in February 1937 and boasted such novelties as a retractable undercarriage and enclosed cockpit. In a 1938 *Regia Aeronautica* fly-off against the Macchi MC.200, the Fiat proved slower but was more manoeuvrable and was declared the winner, though both types received production orders.

The second prototype G.50, pictured, was first flown at Pisa in October 1937 but was lost in a fatal accident on its sixth flight.

Fiat G.50

Weight: 2402kg (5296lb)
Dimensions: Length 8.01m (26ft 3in), Wingspan 10.99m (36ft 1in), Height 3.28m (10ft 9in)
Powerplant: One 649kW (870hp) Fiat A.74 R.C.38 14-cylinder air-cooled radial piston engine

Maximum speed: 470km/h (290mph)
Range: 445km (277 miles)
Ceiling: 10,700m (35,100ft)
Crew: 1
Armament: Two 12.7mm (0.5in) Breda-SAFAT machine guns

Opposite:
This G.50bis was based at Ursel, Belgium, in October 1940 for operations against the United Kingdom as part of the 56° Stormo Caccia Terrestre.

Right & below:
Although the 1° Gruppo Sperimentale of 12 G.50s were sent to Spain to be tested under operational conditions, they were little used, saw no combat and were passed to the Spanish Air Force at the end of hostilities.

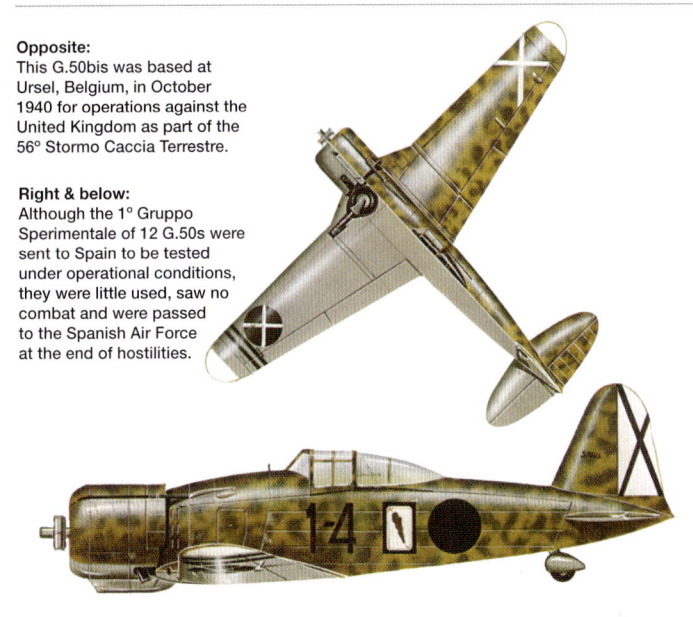

In the same year some of the first production aircraft were sent to Spain for operational trials but in the event the G.50 saw no combat in Spain and the aircraft's first action was over Corsica in Italy's brief campaign against France in June 1940. By this point the enclosed cockpit had been discarded as it was difficult to operate in an emergency and thus pilots had taken to flying with it locked open.

North African success

Committed to the Battle of Britain, the G.50 scored no victories due to its inadequate speed, allowing British aircraft to easily evade it, but enjoyed more success over North Africa and in Greece. It was increasingly used as a fighter-bomber and was the most numerous Italian aircraft used to attack the Allied landings in Sicily. By contrast, its service in Finland, where it was in service from 1939, was outstanding. Finnish pilots managed to shoot down 99 Soviet aircraft for the loss of just three Fiats and the G.50 remained frontline equipment until September 1944.

Fiat G.55 *Centauro*

> **Considered by many the finest Italian fighter of the war, the G.55 possessed outstanding handling, performance and armament but was built in comparatively small numbers.**

Fiat's successor to the mediocre G.50 flew in April 1942, powered by a licence-built DB 605. Excellent performance and handling led to a *Regia Aeronautica* order for 2400 aircraft. In the event, only 35 would be delivered by the armistice but the head of a German commission that tested Italian fighters during February 1943 described the G.55 as the 'the best fighter in the Axis', though plans

Had the war progressed differently, it is likely that the impressive DB 603-powered G.56 would have entered production.

Fiat G.55/I *Centauro*

Weight: 3718kg (8197lb)
Dimensions: Length 9.37m (30ft 9in), Wingspan 11.85m (38ft 11in), Height 3.13m (10ft 3in)
Powerplant: One 1085kW (1455hp) Fiat RA.1050 R.C.58 Tifone ('Typhoon') inverted V-12 liquid-cooled piston engine (licence-built Daimler-Benz DB 605A-1)
Maximum speed: 623km/h (387mph)

Range: 1200km (750 miles)
Ceiling: 12,750m (41,800ft)
Crew: 1
Armament: One engine-mounted and two wing-mounted 20mm (0.79in) MG 151/20 cannon and two 12.7mm (0.5in) Breda-SAFAT machine guns in the upper engine cowling, provision for two 160kg (350lb) bombs

Opposite:
Most of the G.55s that saw action flew, like 'Red 6', with the ANR, the air force of Mussolini's Italian Social Republic puppet state.

Above & below:
'Yellow 1' was based at Bresso, near Milan, in April 1944 and bears the insignia of 2° Gruppo, *Diavoli Rossi* ('Red Devils') on the nose.

to build the G.55 in Germany ultimately came to nothing. Used in the defence of Rome during the summer of 1943, the three 20mm (0.79in) cannon of the *Centauro* ('Centaur') supplemented by two 12.7mm (0.5in) machine guns, representing a terrific punch for a single-engine fighter, combined with its excellent altitude performance proved effective against USAF bombers.

ANR fighter

After its brief *Regia Aeronautica* service, many examples were confiscated by the *Luftwaffe* but the G.55 remained in production at Fiat's Turin factory and continued to be used by the fascist *Aeronautica Nazionale Repubblicana* (ANR). Ultimately 274 examples were built during the war and the *Centauro* formed the equipment of four ANR frontline fighter squadrons. Unusually for an Axis fighter, production of the G.55 continued after the war with some Syrian and Egyptian examples seeing combat against Israel in 1948.

Macchi MC.200 *Saetta*

A contemporary of the Fiat G.50, the Macchi MC.200 proved to be the better aircraft and was built in greater numbers.

Designed by Mario Castoldi who had been responsible for several successful racing seaplanes to compete in the Schneider Trophy races, the somewhat rotund MC.200 *Saetta* ('Lightning Bolt') bore little obvious outward sign of its racing heritage and its top speed of around 500km/h (310mph) was not exactly outstanding by the time it made its maiden flight in December 1937. Early

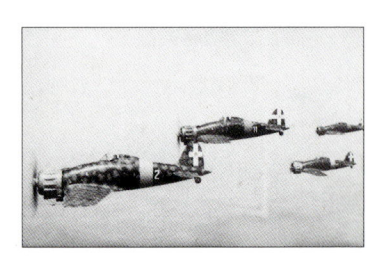

MC.200s of 22º *Gruppo* fly in loose formation over Ukraine during the late summer of 1941.

Macchi MC.200 *Saetta*

Weight: 2395kg (5280lb)
Dimensions: Length 8.25m (27ft 1in), Wingspan 10.58m (34ft 9in), Height 3.05m (10ft 0in)
Powerplant: One 649kW (870hp) Fiat A.74 R.C.38 14-cylinder air-cooled radial piston engine

Maximum speed: 504km/h (313mph)
Range: 570km (350 miles)
Ceiling: 8900m (29,200ft)
Crew: 1
Armament: 12.7mm (0.5in) Breda-SAFAT machine guns; up to 300kg (660lb) bombload under wings on later aircraft

Opposite:
Early production MC.200 fitted with the unpopular enclosed cockpit. This aircraft is with the 371° *Squadriglia*, 22° *Gruppo* 'Cucaracha' in late 1940.

Above:
Serving with the 86° *Squadriglia*, 7° *Gruppo*, 54° *Stormo*, this MC.200 sports the interim windscreen design and features the tiger's head badge of the 54° *Stormo*.

Below:
Fitted with the definitive windscreen arrangement, this *Falco* was operating with the 373° *Squadriglia* of 153° *Gruppo Autonomo* at Puglia, Italy, in 1941.

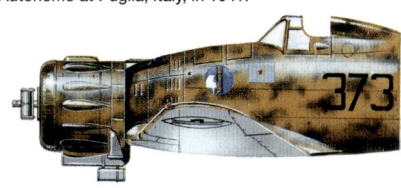

MC.200s featured an enclosed cockpit but this feature, as on the Fiat G.50, was soon discarded. Initial problems with poor spin recovery were solved and the MC.200 was noted for its superlative handling and lack of vices.

North African campaign

Appearing too late to be sent to the conflict in Spain, the MC.200 made its combat debut in the Mediterranean, scoring its first victory, a Short Sunderland flying boat, near Sicily on 1 November 1940. Further action followed over Malta and North Africa, where it was the most numerous Italian fighter, the type proving effective against the Hawker Hurricane, which, though marginally faster, could not match the MC.200's manoeuvrability. The MC.200 also served on the Eastern Front where it was used both in air combat and for ground attack and was credited with 88 'kills'. With more capable fighters emerging, the *Saetta* operated as a fighter-bomber and trainer, continuing in the latter role until 1947.

Macchi MC.202 *Folgore*

Essentially consisting of a *Saetta* airframe mated to a licence-built DB 601 engine, the sleek MC.202 brought Italian fighter performance up to world standard.

Work on the MC.202 began in January 1940 when the Macchi company imported a Daimler-Benz DB 601 at their own expense, before licence production of this engine had begun at Alfa Romeo, in order to adapt the MC.200 to accept this engine in place of the usual Fiat radial. The prototype made its first flight on 10 August 1940 and test pilots were delighted to find that despite its much improved

This MC.202 is wearing the markings of the Co-Belligerent Air Force that flew alongside the Allies from 1943.

Macchi MC.202CB *Folgore*

Weight: 2930kg (6460lb)
Dimensions: Length 8.85m (29ft 0in), Wingspan 10.58m (34ft 9in), Height 3.49m (11ft 5in)
Powerplant: One 864kW (1159hp) Alfa Romeo RA.1000 R.C.41-I Monsone ('Monsoon') inverted V-12 liquid-cooled piston engine (licence-built Daimler-Benz DB 601)

Maximum speed: 600km/h (370mph)
Range: 765km (475 miles)
Ceiling: 11,500m (37,700ft)
Crew: 1
Armament: Two 12.7mm (0.5in) Breda-SAFAT machine guns in the engine cowling and two 7.7mm (0.303in) Breda-SAFAT machine guns in the wings, up to 320kg (700lb) bombload

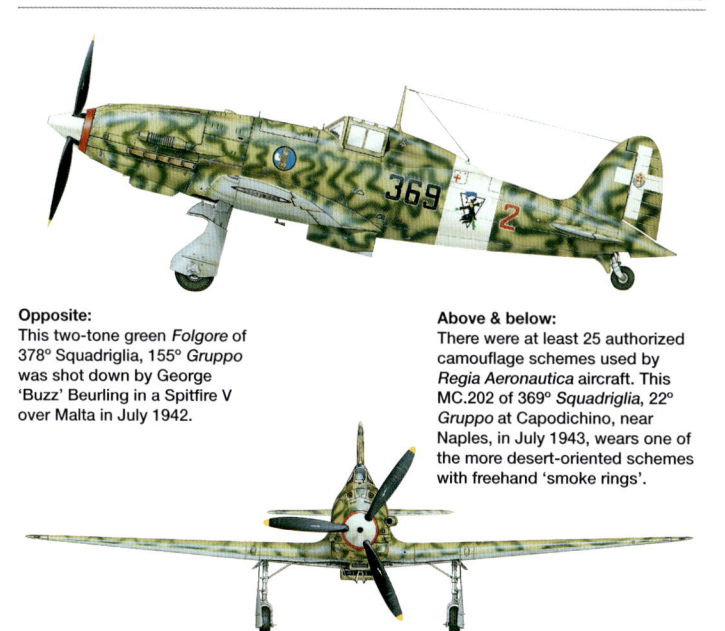

Opposite:
This two-tone green *Folgore* of 378º Squadriglia, 155º *Gruppo* was shot down by George 'Buzz' Beurling in a Spitfire V over Malta in July 1942.

Above & below:
There were at least 25 authorized camouflage schemes used by *Regia Aeronautica* aircraft. This MC.202 of 369º *Squadriglia*, 22º *Gruppo* at Capodichino, near Naples, in July 1943, wears one of the more desert-oriented schemes with freehand 'smoke rings'.

performance, the *Folgore* ('Lightning') had largely retained the excellent handling of the *Saetta*. Rushed into service in mid 1941, early production MC.202s suffered a litany of teething issues but the combat effectiveness of the aircraft was immediately clear, proving superior to both the Hawker Hurricane and Curtiss P-40 in both performance and handling.

Extra armament

The armament of just two machine guns was recognized as inadequate from the start and would prove a particular handicap when the Spitfire, possessing similar performance but far more heavily armed, was introduced to Malta in early 1942. Later *Folgores* added wing guns but the fighter was never well armed by international standards. Like the MC.200, the MC.202 served for a time against the USSR and around 20 were supplied to Croatia. Virtually all of Italy's most successful fighter pilots flew the *Folgore* for some or all of their career.

Macchi MC.205 *Veltro*

A development of the MC.202 with the Daimler-Benz DB 605 engine, the *Veltro* was the ultimate Macchi fighter to see service during the war.

Of the three *Serie V* fighters that were designed to take the DB 605 engine, the MC.205 was officially rated the least promising but as a modification of an existing type was comparatively easy to put into production compared with the more impressive but complicated Fiat G.55 and Reggiane Re.2005. As such, the MC.205 was in service in numbers more quickly and would see more action than the other

This Macchi MC.205 wears the typical 'smoke rings' camouflage of the Italian air force.

Macchi MC.205V *Veltro*

Weight: 3900kg (8598lb)
Dimensions: Length 8.85m (29ft 0in), Wingspan 10.58m (34ft 9in), Height 3.04m (10ft 0in)
Powerplant: One 1085kW (1455hp) Fiat RA.1050 R.C.58 Tifone inverted V-12 liquid-cooled piston engine (licence-built Daimler-Benz DB 605A-1)

Maximum speed: 642km/h (399mph)
Range: 950km (590 miles)
Ceiling: 11,500m (37,700ft)
Crew: 1
Armament: Two 12.7mm (0.5in) Breda-SAFAT machine guns in the nose and two 20mm (0.79in) MG 151 cannon in the wings; up to 320kg (700lb) bombload under wings

Opposite:
This MC.205V was flown by ace Adriano Visconti, commander of the 1° Squadriglia, 1° *Gruppo Caccia*, of the ANR at Campoformido, near Udine, Italy, April 1944.

Above:
One of the Veltros to see *Regia Aeronautica* service before the 1943 armistice, this example wears the badge of the 1° *Stormo Caccia Terrestre*.

Left: An MC.205 *Veltro* in Italian air force markings, before the armistice.

two designs. Retaining the exemplary handling of the earlier Macchi fighters, the *Veltro* ('Greyhound') benefitted from the considerable leap in power offered by the DB 605 and coupled it, somewhat belatedly, with acceptable firepower, and the aircraft quickly gained respect for its outstanding combat performance.

Flying for both sides

Arriving in combat units in February 1943, the MC.205 saw more *Regia Aeronautica* service than the other *Serie V* fighters. After the September armistice, MC.205s continued in service with both the fascist ANR in the north of Italy with a handful becoming part of the Italian Co-Belligerent Air Force, fighting alongside the Allies. Just over 20 examples were also operated by the *Luftwaffe* and an unknown number supplied to Croatia. After the war the MC.205 saw combat again with Egypt against Israel in 1948 and remained in Italian service until 1955, latterly as a training aircraft.

Reggiane Re.2000 and MAVAG Héja

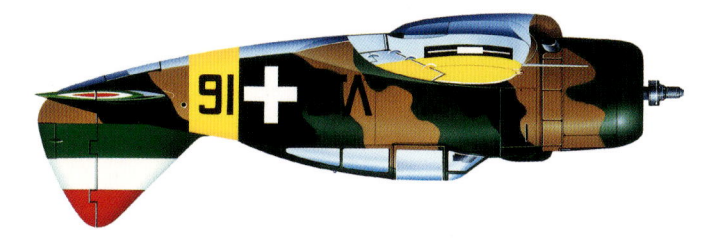

A modern fighter of respectable performance, the Re.2000 was nonetheless rejected by the *Regia Aeronautica* but operated in numbers with Hungary and Sweden.

Designed with a strong American influence, the Re.2000 boasted superior performance to the MC.200 and G.50 but was rejected for service on the grounds that its fuel tanks, contained in the wings as an integral part of the wing design (a so-called 'wet-wing') and not self-sealing separate tanks, would be too vulnerable to battle damage. Despite this, a small number of Re.2000s did

This aircraft was one of several Re.2000s commandeered from the Hungarian export batch for *Regia Aeronautica* service.

Reggiane Re.2000

Weight: 2839kg (6259lb)

Dimensions: Length 7.99m (26ft 3in), Wingspan 11m (36ft 1in), Height 3.2m (10ft 6in)

Powerplant: One 735kW (986hp) Piaggio P.XI R.C.40 14-cylinder air-cooled radial piston engine

Maximum speed: 530km/h (330mph)

Range: 545km (339 miles)

Ceiling: 11,200m (36,700ft)

Crew: 1

Armament: Two 12.7mm (0.5in) Breda-SAFAT machine guns in the upper cowling

Opposite:
Hungarian-built MAVAG *Heja II*, which differed greatly from the original Re.2000, not least in its use of a Weiss Manfréd WM K-14B engine.

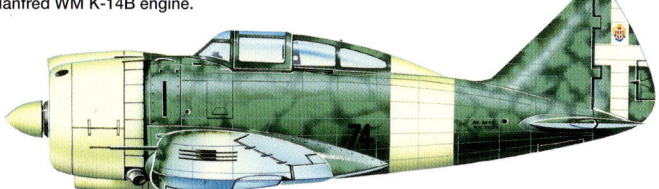

Above:
One of the first five production machines, this Re.2000 was with the Sezione Sperimentale (Experimental Section) of 74ª Squadriglia, Comiso, Sicily, in spring 1941.

Below:
As an emergency measure, the Swedish Air Force purchased 60 Re.2000 Serie Is, under the designation J 20.

serve with the *Regia Aeronautica* in Sicily, mainly on long-range escort missions. The Italian Navy also adopted the aircraft for catapult use aboard its capital ships, though lacking any means to recover the aircraft, the pilot was forced to seek a shore-based location to land.

Hungarian service

But the main user of the Re.2000 was Hungary, which obtained 70 examples before obtaining a manufacturing licence to build around 200 of an improved version at the MAVAG factory as the *Héja* ('Hawk'). The *Héja* served on the Eastern Front until January 1943 and performed satisfactorily in combat against Soviet fighters thanks to its excellent manoeuvrability. Sweden operated 60 Re.2000s, using them to intercept aircraft violating Swedish airspace, losing one in combat to a Dornier Do 24 in early April 1945.

Reggiane Re.2001 *Falco II*

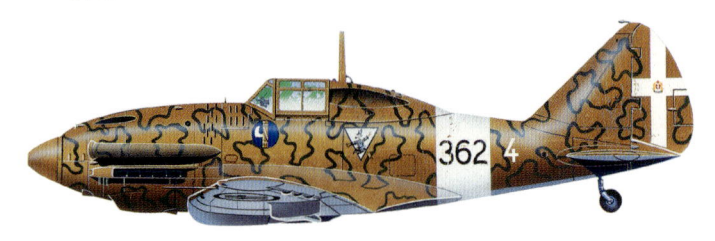

> Derived from the Re.2000, the Re.2001 solved the two major problems that afflicted its progenitor but delays kept it from being built in large numbers.

The most obvious change adopted by the Re.2001 was its engine. The Re.2000's Piaggio radial of dubious reliability was replaced by the Alfa Romeo *Monsone* ('Monsoon'), a licence-built DB 601 that was both reliable and delivered greater power. Most of the rear fuselage was unchanged from the earlier machine but internally a fuel tank was now included in the fuselage though much

An Re.2001 fighter in Co-Belligerent markings with green and red roundels.

Reggiane Re.2001/III *Falco II*

Weight: 3280kg (7231lb)
Dimensions: Length 8.36m (27ft 5in), Wingspan 11m (36ft 1in), Height 3.15m (10ft 4in)
Powerplant: One 864kW (1159hp) Alfa Romeo RA.1000 R.C.41-I Monsone inverted V-12 liquid-cooled piston engine (licence-built Daimler-Benz DB 601)

Maximum speed: 542km/h (337mph)
Range: 1100km (680 miles)
Ceiling: 11,000m (36,000ft)
Crew: 1
Armament: Two 2.7mm (0.5in) Breda-SAFAT machine guns in upper cowling and two 7.7mm (0.303in) Breda-SAFAT machine guns in wings

Opposite:
Based at Capodichino, Naples, in August 1942, this Re.2001 wears the emblem of 22° Gruppo *Spauracchio* ('Scarecrow').

Above & right:
Only nine Re.2001s remained serviceable at the time of the September armistice and eight joined the Co-Belligerent Air Force. This one was part of the 82ª *Squadriglia*, 21° *Gruppo* based at Puglia in late 1943.

time was lost when the *Regia Aeronautica* decreed that the new aircraft must carry all its fuel in the wings, leading to a significant redesign of the wing's internal structure.

Pilots' favourite

Re.2001s began to be delivered to combat units in late 1941, approximately a year late, and the aircraft received praise from its pilots for its outstanding manoeuvrability, said to be superior to the contemporary MC.202 and demonstrably superior to the Spitfire. It was, however, slower than the Macchi aircraft, and most of its opponents. Nonetheless, in action over Malta the Re.2001 performed well. The Re.2001CB also proved effective in the fighter-bomber role, and the type was adapted for night fighting. Only 237 Re.2001s were built in total, the rival MC.202 having priority for engine deliveries as well as being significantly cheaper to produce.

Reggiane Re.2002 *Ariete*

A switch back to a radial engine resulted in the Re.2002 which boasted excellent performance and was used to great effect as a fighter-bomber by Italy and Germany.

Consisting of a modified and strengthened Re.2000 fuselage mated to a redesigned wing with conventional fuel tanks, the prototype *Ariete* ('Ram') flew for the first time in March 1942. Intended to be a fighter-bomber, a radial engine was selected for the aircraft as this type of engine, without a potentially vulnerable cooling system, was seen as preferable for the ground attack role. The engine change

The Re.2002 prototype wears the typical markings of Italian aircraft before the September 1943 armistice.

Reggiane Re.2002 *Ariete*

Weight: 3240kg (7143lb)
Dimensions: Length 8.16m (26ft 9in), Wingspan 11.0m (36ft 1in), Height 3.15m (10ft 4in)
Powerplant: One 876kW (1175hp) Piaggio P.XIX R.C.45 Turbine 14-cylinder air-cooled radial piston engine
Maximum speed: 530km/h (330mph)

Range: 1100km (680 miles)
Ceiling: 11,000m (36,000ft)
Crew: 1
Armament: Two 2.7mm (0.5in) Breda-SAFAT machine guns in upper cowling and two 7.7mm (0.303in) Breda-SAFAT machine guns in wings; up to 650kg (1430lb) bombload under fuselage and wings

Opposite:
As yet unpainted with unit markings, this *Luftwaffe* Re.2002 was awaiting delivery to a *Schlachtgruppe* squadron at Toliedo, near Milan, in 1945.

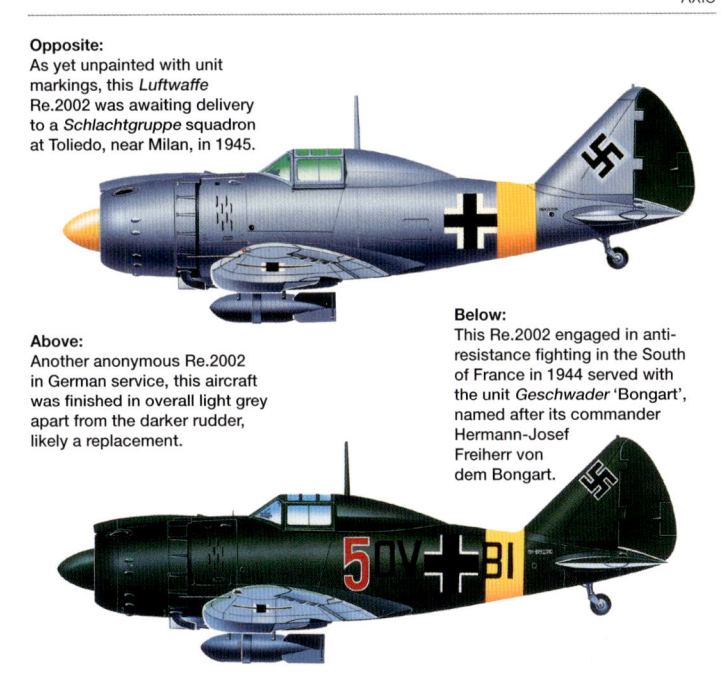

Above:
Another anonymous Re.2002 in German service, this aircraft was finished in overall light grey apart from the darker rudder, likely a replacement.

Below:
This Re.2002 engaged in anti-resistance fighting in the South of France in 1944 served with the unit *Geschwader* 'Bongart', named after its commander Hermann-Josef Freiherr von dem Bongart.

also sidestepped production issues that were bedevilling deliveries of the licence-built version of German inline engines. The Piaggio *Turbine* engine was a new design, however, and teething troubles afflicted the aircraft in early service.

Fighter-bomber

The Re.2002 proved to be an excellent fighter-bomber possessing good speed and manoeuvrability and carrying a heavy bombload, by Italian standards at least. Deliveries of the new aircraft began in March 1942 and the first batch of 100 was delivered by July, the same month that the Allies initiated Operation Husky, the invasion of Sicily, and the Re.2002 saw much action attacking Allied landing forces though losses were heavy. After the September armistice, the aircraft formed the equipment of one Co-Belligerent Air Force squadron and was used to attack German shipping. Meanwhile, the *Luftwaffe* requisitioned 60 Re.2002s, operating them in Southern France.

Reggiane Re.2005 *Sagittario*

> The final Reggiane fighter design was produced in trivial numbers, but during its brief service proved to be one of the finest fighters in the world.

Superficially resembling a stretched Re.2001, the *Sagittario* ('Sagittarius') was in fact a clean sheet design, owing little to the earlier aircraft. The prototype, powered by an imported DB 605, was flown on 9 May 1942 and unusually for a prototype was later used in combat, intercepting a USAF bombing raid on Naples. Testing revealed that the flying qualities of the Re.2005 were the finest of the *Serie V*

A Reggiane Re.2005 on the tarmac of an unidentified airfield. An Re.2001 is visible in the background.

Reggiane Re.2005 *Sagittario*

Weight: 3610kg (7959lb)
Dimensions: Length 8.73m (28ft 8in), Wingspan 11m (36ft 1in), Height 3.15m (10ft 4in)
Powerplant: One 1085kW (1455hp) Fiat RA.1050 R.C.58 Tifone inverted V-12 liquid-cooled piston engine (licence-built Daimler-Benz DB 605A-1)
Maximum speed: 628km/h (390mph)

Range: 980km (610 miles)
Ceiling: 11,500m (37,700ft)
Crew: 1
Armament: One 20mm (0.79in) MG 151 cannon firing through propeller hub and two MG 151 cannon in wings, plus two 12.7mm (0.5in) Breda-SAFAT machine guns in upper cowling; up to 320kg (700lb) bombs under wings

Opposite & above:
Only six of the Re.2005s to survive until the September armistice entered service with the fascist ANR and these were used as advanced trainers.

Right: First flown in May 1942, only 54 examples of the Re.2005 had been built when Italy withdrew from the war in September 1943.

fighters, especially at altitude, but it was expensive and complicated to build so the marginally less impressive G.55 was favoured for future production for the *Regia Aeronautica*. However, recognizing the type's excellence, an order was nevertheless placed for 750 Re.2005s.

Sicily campaign

In the event only 54 were constructed and only one unit was ever wholly equipped with the *Sagittario,* flying the Re.2005 from April 1943 until the armistice, engaging in the heavy fighting over Sicily. The main fighter opponent of the Re.2005 was the Spitfire Mk.IX and the two aircraft were well matched in the air, with individual combats often decided by pilot skill. After the armistice, 13 Re.2005s were seized by Germany, though details of any operational service with the *Luftwaffe* remain unknown.

Kawanishi N1K1-J and -2J *Shiden* 'George'

The most formidable Imperial Japanese Navy (IJN) fighter to enter production, the *Shiden* was the equal of any Allied fighter and an extremely dangerous foe in the hands of an experienced pilot.

Kawanishi specialized in the production of flying boats and the *Shiden* ('Violet Lightning') originally derived from the fighter floatplane the N1K1 'Rex', which was built in small numbers and saw some combat in South East Asia. As a private venture, Kawanishi removed the cumbersome float from the N1K1 to produce a landplane fighter which proved faster than the A6M and longer ranged than

A Kawanishi N1K2-Ja Shiden Kai. The type was mainly used against the USAF's B-29 bomber offensive.

Kawanishi N1K1-J

Weight: 4321kg (9526lb)
Dimensions: Length 8.89m (29ft 2in), Wingspan 12m (39ft 4in), Height 4.06m (13ft 4in)
Powerplant: One 1473kW (1975hp) Nakajima NK9H Homare 21 18-cylinder air-cooled radial piston engine

Maximum speed: 571km/h (355mph)
Range: 1078km (670 miles)
Ceiling: 12,009m (39,400ft)
Crew: 1
Armament: Four 20mm (0.79in) Type 99 Mark 2 machine guns in the wings; up to 500kg (1100lb) bombload under wings

Opposite:
This aircraft served with the unit most associated with the Kawanishi fighter, the elite 343rd Naval Air Group commanded by Minoru Genda.

Above (both images):
This modified Kawanishi N1K2-J, Yo 104, belonged to the Yokosuka Air Group, based at Yokosuka Air Base in February 1945. This aircraft was assigned to Warrant Officer Kaneyoshi Mutoh, who is credited with around 30 kills, including four F6F Hellcats in a single combat on 16 February 1945.

the J2M and was thus hastily put into production as the N1K1-J. Problems were experienced with the long undercarriage (a hangover from the mid-wing configuration of the N1K1) and the *Homare* engine but when it worked properly the aircraft was outstanding in both performance and manoeuvrability.

Lighter type

Later the design was thoroughly reworked by Kawanishi, resulting in the N1K2-J, which was a quarter of a tonne lighter and solved the undercarriage problem by moving the entire wing to a lower position on the fuselage. The whole airframe was simplified and could be built in fewer man hours but unfortunately for the IJN the Kawanishi factory was bombed by B-29s and only 415 N1K2-Js were produced compared to 1007 of the earlier N1K1-J. The *Shiden* formed the equipment of the elite 343 *Kokutai* ('Naval Air Group'), which proved highly successful in combat during the closing days of the war.

Kawasaki Ki-45 *Toryu* 'Nick'

Designed as a long-range bomber escort, the Ki-45 subsequently operated in a variety of roles, achieving considerable success as a night fighter.

The vogue for twin-engine 'heavy' fighters, developed at the end of the 1930s, found its expression in Japan in the form of the *Toryu* ('Dragonslayer') which first flew in January 1939. Major developmental problems led to a time consuming near total redesign to become the Ki-45-KAI which entered production in September 1941, with deliveries beginning to service units in August

*Toryu*s of the 53rd Sentai, based at Matsudo near Tokyo. The twin 20mm (0.79in) Ho-5 cannon firing forward and upward can be seen in the foreground aircraft.

Kawasaki Ki-45-KAI-Hei *Toryu*

Weight: 8820kg (19,445lb)
Dimensions: Length 11m (36ft 1in), Wingspan 15.02m (49ft 3in), Height 3.7m (12ft 2in)
Powerplant: Two 805kW (1080hp) Mitsubishi Ha-102 14-cylinder air-cooled radial piston engines
Maximum speed: 547km/h (340mph)
Range: 2000km (1200 miles)

Ceiling: 10,730m (35,200ft)
Crew: 2
Armament: One 37mm (1.46in) Ho-203 cannon firing through ventral tunnel, two 20mm (0.79in) Ho-5 cannon firing obliquely upwards and forwards, one 7.92mm (0.31in) Type 98 machine gun flexibly mounted in rear cockpit (early aircraft only)

Opposite:
A Ki-45-KAI-Hei of the 2nd *Chutai*, 27th *Sentai*.
Originally a light bomber unit, the 27th converted to the
Toryu for operations over Malaya and the Philippines.

Above:
This Ki-45-KAI-Ko was flown
by the 1st *Sentai*, 5th *Chutai*, in
1943. The 5th *Chutai* was the
first unit to operate the *Toryu*
and saw much action in New
Guinea and the Philippines.

Below:
Used by the Headquarters
Chutai of the 21st Sentai in May
1945, this Ki-45-KAI-Hei was
based at Palembang, Sumatra.

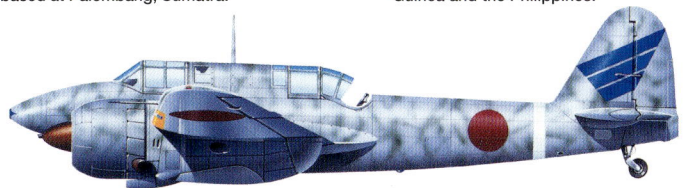

1942. Although possessing excellent manoeuvrability and handling for an
aircraft of its size, when committed to its intended role of bomber escort the
Ki-45, like the contemporary Bf 110, proved no match for single-engined
fighters but found much more success as a ground-attack, anti-shipping and
bomber-interceptor aircraft.

Night fighter

In the latter role, as US bombing activities increasingly took place at night, so
the Ki-45 was compelled to operate as a night fighter and the Ki-45-KAI-Hei
was developed specifically for nocturnal operations. This aircraft featured a
37mm (1.46in) cannon firing forwards as well as two 20mm (0.79in) weapons
firing obliquely upwards in the same manner as the *Schräge Musik* installation in
German night fighters and proved effective against the B-24. A centimetric radar
set was planned to be fitted in the nose but this had not been developed by the
end of the war and no Ki-45 was ever equipped with radar.

Kawasaki Ki-102 'Randy'

Kawasaki's replacement for the Ki-45, the Ki-102 was an impressive performer but saw little action as most examples were held in reserve.

Flying for the first time in March 1944, the Ki-102 resembled a scaled up Ki-45. The wings and tail were taken from a single-seat prototype, the Ki-96, that Kawasaki had flown in 1943 and which had demonstrated excellent performance but was not serially produced. The Ki-102 was originally intended to operate as an attack craft and strike fighter but by the time it appeared B-29 raids on the Japanese

The Ki-102 derived from the Ki-96 single-seater, pictured, which did not enter production as Army policy required a second crewmember.

Kawasaki Ki-102-Otsu

Weight: 7300kg (16,094lb)
Dimensions: Length 11.45m (37ft 7in), Wingspan 15.57m (51ft 1in), Height 3.7m (12ft 2in)
Powerplant: 1120kW (1500hp) Mitsubishi Ha112-II Ru 14-cylinder air-cooled radial engines
Maximum speed: 580km/h (360mph)

Range: 2000km (1200 miles)
Ceiling: 10,000m (33,000ft)
Crew: 2
Armament: One 37mm (1.46in) Ho-204 cannon in nose and two 20mm (0.79in) Ho-5 cannon in lower fuselage, optional two Ho-5 cannon firing obliquely upwards; up to 500kg (1100lb) bombload or one Ki-148 guided missile

Opposite & below:
This Ki-102-Otsu was on the strength of the 3rd *Chutai* of the 45th *Sentai*, a unit that had previously flown the Ki-45, based at Hokota, Japan, in August 1945.

A captured Ki-102-Ko in USAAF markings, one of three shipped to the US for flight testing, all of which had been scrapped by 1950.

mainland were imminent and Kawasaki was asked to modify six pre-production airframes into interceptors. Flight testing revealed the Ki-102 possessed excellent performance and exemplary handling but production was delayed due to bombing of Kawasaki's Akashi factory.

In total, 215 Ki-102s were delivered to the Army, but few of these saw combat. Those that did were issued piecemeal to Ki-45 units and used to intercept B-29 raids. A handful of the Ki-102-Ko variant, featuring turbo-supercharged engines, also made it into service, one pre-production example destroying three B-29s in the hands of ace Yasohiko Kuroe. Most Ki-102s, however, were not committed to combat and were intended to deliver the Ki-148 air-to-surface radio guided missile against the expected Allied invasion. By the end of the war two prototypes of a pressurized single-seat derivative developed specifically to intercept the high flying B-29, the Ki-108, had begun flight testing but did not enter production.

Kawasaki Ki-61 *Hien* 'Tony'

The only Japanese fighter of World War II to enter service equipped with an inline engine, the Ki-61 was also notable for its sturdy construction and excellent performance.

Kawasaki had obtained a licence to produce the Daimler-Benz DB 601 (as the Ha-40) and the first Japanese-built engine was run in July 1941. The Ki-61, powered by one of the first production engines, subsequently made its first flight in December of the same year. The *Hien* ('Flying Swallow') differed from previous Japanese Army fighters in providing some protection for the pilot as well as self-sealing

A Ki-61-1-Otsu of the 37th *Sentai* based at Taipei, Formosa (now Taiwan), in early 1945.

Kawasaki Ki-61-I-KAIc

Weight: 3470kg (7650lb)
Dimensions: Length 8.94m (29ft 4in), Wingspan 12m (39ft 4in), Height 3.7m (12ft 2in)
Powerplant: One 864kW (1159hp) Kawasaki Ha-40 inverted V-12 liquid-cooled piston engine (licence-built Daimler-Benz DB601)
Maximum speed: 580km/h (360mph)

Range: 580km (360 miles)
Ceiling: 11,600m (38,100ft)
Crew: 1
Armament: Two 20mm (0.79in) Ho-5 cannon in wings and 12.7mm (0.5in) Ho-103 machine guns in upper fuselage nose; up to 500kg (1100lb) bombload under wings

Opposite:
Serving with the 1st *Chutai*, 55th *Sentai*, at Chofu, Tokyo, in late 1944, this Ki-61-I-KAI-Hei was previously with the 53rd *Sentai*, Hence the overpainted tail insignia.

Above:
On Okinawa in late 1944 or early 1945, this Ki-61-I-KAI-Hei has had field-applied camouflage painted, somewhat crudely, on the fuselage sides. It was serving with the 19th *Sentai*.

Below:
This Ki-61-I-Otsu of the 3rd *Chutai*, 59th *Sentai* based at Ashiya, Japan, features a replacement rudder with the badge of a different unit partly painted upon it.

fuel tanks. Entering service in the New Guinea campaign, the first Allied pilots who encountered the Ki-61 assumed it must be an imported German or Italian type and the 'Tony' reporting name was apparently adopted because of its resemblance to contemporary Italian fighters.

Air superiority

In combat the Ki-61 proved effective, outclassing the P-40, the most numerous type in the theatre, and demonstrating dive performance and a resistance to battle damage unknown in any previous Japanese fighter. Luckily for the Allies, the Ki-61 suffered from severe engine reliability issues restricting its combat availability. Despite these issues the Ha-40 was developed into the more powerful Ha-140 which promised better altitude performance and powered the second-generation Ki-61-II but a January 1945 B-29 raid destroyed Kawasaki's Akashi engine factory and only around 30 Ki-61-IIs were completed.

Kawasaki Ki-100

Few fighters have made a change from inline to radial engine (or vice versa), fewer still with such unequivocal success as the Ki-100, possibly the Imperial Army's finest late-war fighter.

Kawasaki's engine production had never kept pace with that of airframes and by the end of 1944, 200 Ki-61 airframes were stored outdoors awaiting engines. Then, on 19 January 1945, a B-29 raid on Kawasaki's Akashi plant effectively brought engine production to an end. The decision to re-engineer the Ki-61 to accept the radial Ha-112 engine, which was in relatively plentiful supply and

This Kawasaki Ki-100-I-Otsu flew as part of the 5th Sentai.

Kawasaki Ki-100-I-Ko

Weight: 3495kg (7705lb)
Dimensions: Length 8.82m (28ft 11in), Wingspan 12m (39ft 4in), Height 3.75m (12ft 4in)
Powerplant: One 1120kW (1500hp) Mitsubishi Ha-112-II 14-cylinder two-row air-cooled radial engine
Maximum speed: 580km/h (360mph)

Range: 1400km (870 miles) on internal fuel
Ceiling: 11,000m (36,000ft)
Crew: 1
Armament: Two 20mm (0.79in) Ho-5 cannon in wings and 12.7mm (0.5in) Ho-103 machine guns in upper fuselage nose; up to 500kg (1100lb) bombload under wings

Opposite:
A Ki-100-I-Otsu of the 3rd *Chutai*, 59th *Sentai*, based at Ashiya airfield, near Osaka, Japan, in the summer of 1945.

Above:
The 18th *Sentai* operated the Ki-100, such as this Ki-100-I-Ko, in concert with the Ki-61 in early 1945 from Kashiwa, Tokyo. Curiously the Ki-100 never received an Allied reporting name.

Above:
Another 59th *Sentai* aircraft, this Ki-100-I-Ko served the 3rd *Chutai*. The improvement to rearward visibility provided by the cut-down rear fuselage can easily be discerned when one compares this aircraft to the Ki-100-Otsu opposite.

possessed much better reliability, had been authorized in October 1944 but Takeo Doi, chief designer of the Ki-61, expressed doubt that the conversion would be successful as the Ha-112 was 45kg (99lb) lighter than the inline unit, nearly twice as wide and possessed a different thrust line. However, in the absence of any viable alternative, the work went ahead and the resulting Ki-100 proved astonishingly successful.

Tested against a captured P-51C Mustang, the Ki-100 was found to be slower but much more manoeuvrable and could out-dive the American aircraft. Against the F6F Hellcat, the Ki-100 was believed to be superior in every metric. In frontline service from April 1945, the Ki-100 proved formidable and, crucially, reliable. Later examples featured a cut-down rear fuselage for all-round visibility and the aircraft remained in service until VJ day.

Mitsubishi A5M 'Claude'

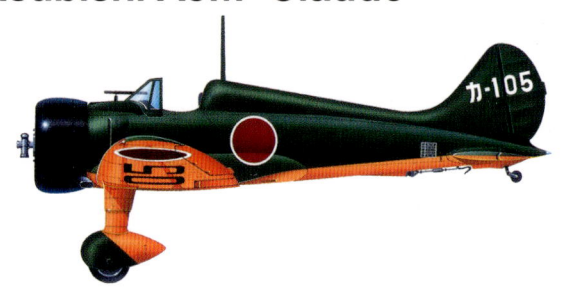

Although in the twilight of its frontline career by 1941, the A5M had already achieved air superiority in the Second Sino-Japanese War and announced Japan as a major player in naval aviation.

The world's first operational cantilever monoplane shipboard fighter, the A5M ushered in a new era of carrier aircraft, hitherto considered the exclusive domain of the biplane. The aircraft was designed to meet a 1934 specification, one of the requirements of which was a maximum speed of 350km/h (220mph) but the aircraft, designated Ka-14 by Mitsubishi, greatly exceeded this figure with a

The '3' prefix in the tailcode of these A5M2s signifies allocation to the 12th *Kokutai*, a unit which saw much action in China during 1938.

Mitsubishi A5M4

Weight: 1671kg (3684lb)
Dimensions: Length 7.57m (24ft 10in), Wingspan 11m (36ft 1in), Height 3.27m (10ft 9in)
Powerplant: One 530kW (710hp) Nakajima Kotobuki 41 or 41 KAI 9-cylinder air-cooled radial piston engine

Maximum speed: 435km/h (270mph)
Range: 1201km (746 miles)
Ceiling: 9800m (32,200ft)
Crew: 1
Armament: Two 7.7mm (0.303in) Type 97 aircraft machine guns in forward cowling; up to 60kg (132lb) bombload under wings

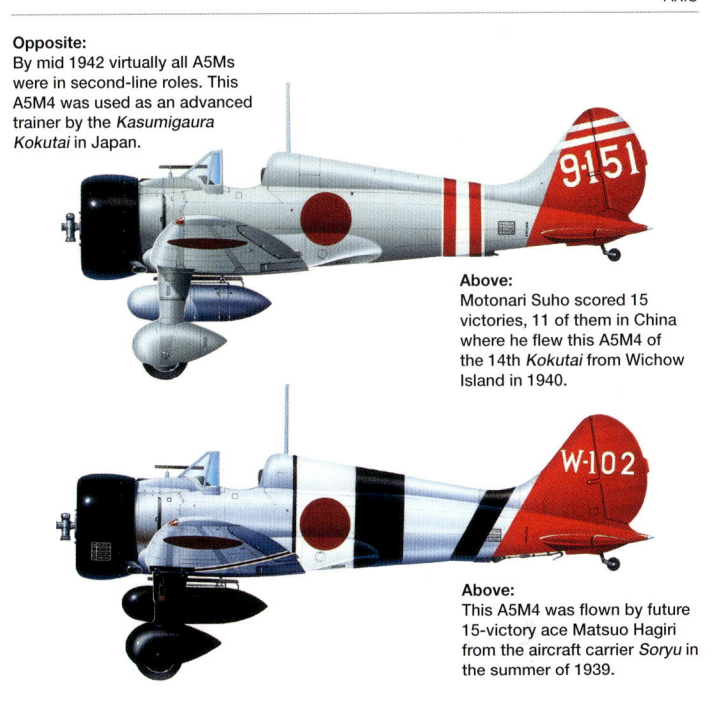

Opposite:
By mid 1942 virtually all A5Ms were in second-line roles. This A5M4 was used as an advanced trainer by the *Kasumigaura Kokutai* in Japan.

Above:
Motonari Suho scored 15 victories, 11 of them in China where he flew this A5M4 of the 14th *Kokutai* from Wichow Island in 1940.

Above:
This A5M4 was flown by future 15-victory ace Matsuo Hagiri from the aircraft carrier *Soryu* in the summer of 1939.

top speed of 450km/h (280mph). Ordered into production as the A5M, the first examples entered service during early 1937. Operations over China saw the A5M pitted against some of the latest fighter types and it gained ascendancy over most of them with relative ease, the exception being the Polikarpov I-16, of similar performance and configuration but boasting a retractable undercarriage, a feature considered for the A5M but rejected due to the weight penalty it would impose.

By the start of World War II the A5M had been replaced on most Japanese carriers but the aircraft remained in frontline service with various units and remained a viable combat aircraft, scoring kills against US aircraft in combat over the Marshall Islands during February 1942. The A5M's last known use as a fighter occurred during the Battle of the Coral Sea in May 1942, after which it was employed as a trainer.

Mitsubishi A6M1–A6M3 *Reisen* 'Zeke'

When it first appeared, the legendary 'Zero' was the finest carrier fighter in the world and proved outstandingly successful throughout the early stages of the Pacific war.

Designed by Jori Horikoshi to an incredibly challenging specification that could only be met if the aircraft were made as light as possible, the Zero was primarily constructed of a new alloy, 'extra super duralumin', developed in 1936. Armour protection and self-sealing fuel tanks were discarded for weight-saving reasons, which gave the Zero both outstanding agility and an incredible

Very few Zeros remain airworthy. This A6M2, re-engined with a Pratt & Whitney R-1830, flew in the 1980s and 90s but is now statically preserved in Hawaii.

Mitsubishi A6M2 Model 21 *Reisen*

Weight: 2796kg (6164lb)
Dimensions: Length 9.06m (29ft 9in), Wingspan 12m (39ft 4in), Height 3.05m (10ft 0in)
Powerplant: One 700kW (940hp) Nakajima NK1C Sakae 12 14-cylinder air-cooled radial piston engine
Maximum speed: 533km/h (331mph)

Range: 1870km (1160 miles)
Ceiling: 10,000m (33,000ft)
Crew: 1
Armament: Two 7.7mm (0.303in) Type 97 aircraft machine guns in engine cowling and 20mm (0.79in) Type 99-1 Mk.3 cannon in the wings; up to 120kg (260lb) bombload under wings

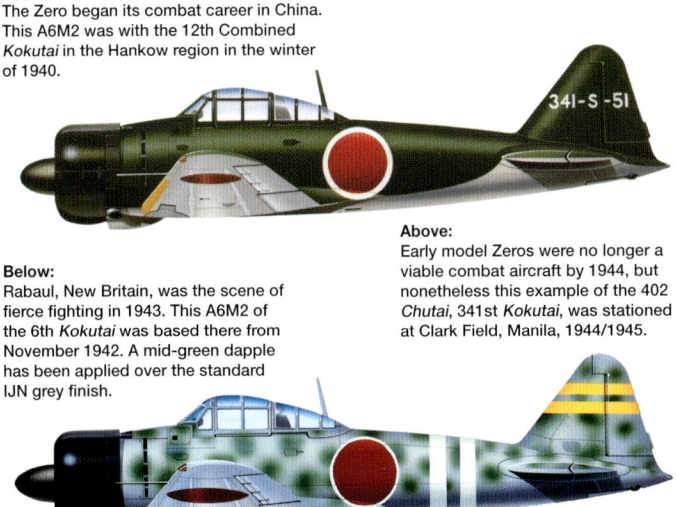

Opposite:
The Zero began its combat career in China. This A6M2 was with the 12th Combined *Kokutai* in the Hankow region in the winter of 1940.

341-S-51

Above:
Early model Zeros were no longer a viable combat aircraft by 1944, but nonetheless this example of the 402 *Chutai*, 341st *Kokutai*, was stationed at Clark Field, Manila, 1944/1945.

Below:
Rabaul, New Britain, was the scene of fierce fighting in 1943. This A6M2 of the 6th *Kokutai* was based there from November 1942. A mid-green dapple has been applied over the standard IJN grey finish.

range performance, but also meant the aircraft was prone to catching fire if hit. The first flight of the A6M1 prototype took place on 1 April 1939 but the Navy requested a switch to the Nakajima Sakae engine, resulting in the A6M2 that comfortably exceeded the specifications and was so promising that the Navy had 15 shipped to China in July 1940 for operational use even before official testing had completed. Over Manchuria the Zero proved utterly dominant. On one occasion, for example, 13 Zeros reportedly shot down 27 I-15s and I-16s in under three minutes without loss.

Pearl Harbor

By the time of the Pearl Harbor attack the Zero was a proven warplane and for the first year or so of the Pacific War appeared invincible until tactics were developed to deal with it. Only minor changes were made to early Zeros, the most significant being a variant with clipped wings to improve rate of roll, designated the A6M3. Nakajima also produced 327 examples of a floatplane fighter, the A6M2-N 'Rufe'.

Mitsubishi A6M5–A6M7 *Reisen* 'Zeke'

As the Zero began to be outclassed by Allied fighters, the A6M5 was developed in an attempt to maintain parity with later designs.

Mitsubishi intended the A6M5 merely to be a stopgap until the A7M *Reppu* entered service but as it turned out the A7M was never produced and the A6M5 remained in production until the end of the conflict, becoming, by a considerable margin, the most produced Zero variant in the process. The main changes were a reduced wingspan, adopted primarily to improve dive performance. The wings

The only airworthy Zero in the world flying with its original Nakajima *Sakae* engine is this A6M5, maintained by the Planes of Fame Museum in California.

Mitsubishi A6M5b Model 52b *Reisen*

Weight: 2733kg (6025lb)
Dimensions: Length 9.12m (29ft 11in), Wingspan 11.0m (36ft 1in), Height 3.50m (11ft 6in)
Powerplant: One 731kW (980hp) Nakajima Sakae 21 14-cylinder air-cooled radial piston engine
Maximum speed: 565km/h (351mph)

Range: 1922km (1194 miles)
Ceiling: 11,740m (38,520ft)
Crew: 1
Armament: One 7.7mm (0.303in) Type 97 aircraft machine gun and one 13.2mm (0.52in) Type 3 aircraft machine gun in upper cowling, two 20mm (0.79in) Type 99 Model 2 Mk.4 cannon in wings; up to 120kg (260lb) bombload

Opposite:
The vibrant orange undersides signify this A6M5 is serving in the training role. It was with the *Genzan Kokutai* based at Wonsan, North Korea, in late 1944.

Right & below:
An example of the A6M5c sub-variant featuring improved armament in the form of an additional pair of 13.2mm (0.52in) machine guns fitted outboard of the standard wing cannon.

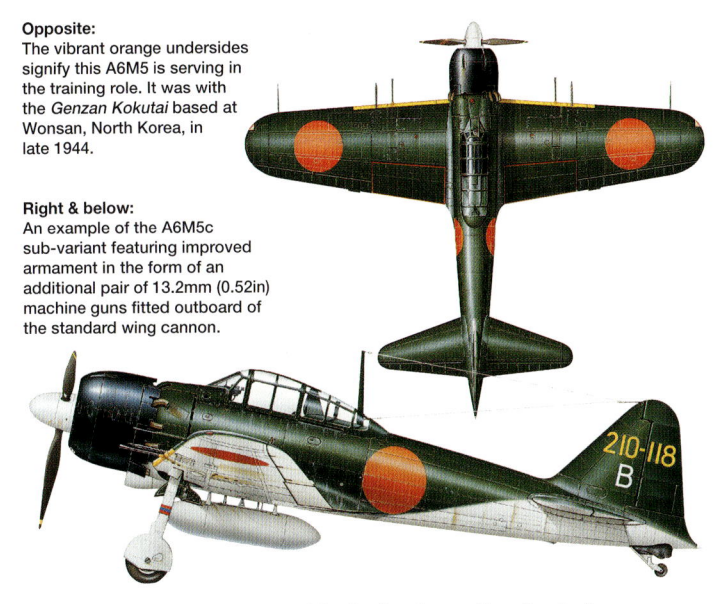

featured a heavier gauge skin and for the first time self-sealing tanks were fitted with later production A6M5s also adopting some armour protection for the pilot. Individual ejector exhausts were adopted to give a measure of thrust augmentation but the change to the Zero's performance was relatively modest.

Late-war limitations

The extent to which the Zero had slipped behind its enemies became apparent when a large number of A6M5b Zeros were committed to the Battle of the Philippine Sea and in combat with the F6F Hellcats of the US Navy the Japanese Navy lost around 350 aircraft in a single day to just 30 US losses, a humiliating defeat that became known as the 'Marianas Turkey Shoot'. Despite this setback, Zero production continued due to the absence of any viable alternative and a final production variant, the A6M7, optimized for the fighter-bomber role, was produced from May 1945 onwards. A total of 10,449 Zeros were built by several companies, making it the most produced Japanese aircraft of all time.

Mitsubishi J2M *Raiden* 'Jack'

Representing a radical departure for the Imperial Navy, the land-based J2M interceptor was designed with an emphasis on speed and rate of climb.

Built to a 1939 specification requiring manoeuvrability to be regarded as secondary to climb and speed, the J2M *Raiden* ('Lightning') with its stubby fuselage mounted on a tiny wing, represented the antithesis of the Zero yet was the work of the same designer, Jori Horikoshi. The initial J2M1 model powered by a fan-cooled Mitsubishi *Kasei* ('Mars') 13 radial engine mounted some distance from

A captured J2M-3 in USAAF markings, is tested by the South West Pacific Area Technical Air Intelligence Unit, April 1945.

Mitsubishi J2M3 *Raiden*

Weight: 3211kg (7079lb)
Dimensions: Length 9.95m (32ft 8in), Wingspan 10.8m (35ft 5in), Height 3.81m (12ft 6in)
Powerplant: One 1300kW (1800hp) Mitsubishi MK4R-A Kasei 23a 14-cylinder air-cooled radial piston engine

Maximum speed: 587km/h (365mph)
Range: 1898km (1179 miles)
Ceiling: 11,700m (38,400ft)
Crew: 1
Armament: Two Type 99 Mk.2 cannon and two Type 99 Mk.1 mounted in wings; up to 120kg (260lb) bombload under wings

Opposite:
The J2M3, Model 21, featured four 20mm (0.79in) cannon, a very heavy armament for a Japanese single-seater. This example was with the 302nd *Kokutai* at Atsugi, Japan, in 1945.

Above & below:
Another 302nd *Kokutai Raiden*, this is a J2M2 model 11 *Raiden* which normally featured two 20mm (0.79in) cannon and two 7.7mm (0.3in) machine guns in the fuselage, but this example has had the machine guns removed and blanked off.

the nose and powering the propeller by an extension shaft failed to meet the Navy's specifications but the J2M2 re-engined with the more powerful *Kasei* 23a engine was ordered into production in October 1942. The aircraft was, however, plagued with developmental issues, with the engine proving particularly troublesome, and delays ensued while the problems were overcome and the *Raiden* finally entered service in December 1943. By this time the J2M3 had entered production with revised armament and this would become the most numerous variant.

Bomber interceptor

In service the *Raiden* was primarily used for combatting B-29 raids, and was rated the best available fighter for this task, being very well armed, though the high altitude at which the Superfortresses flew made interception difficult and much work was carried out to develop a turbo-supercharged J2M4, though this never advanced beyond the prototype stage. The J2M5 however utilised a two-speed mechanically driven supercharger to attain better altitude at the expense of range, a few of which managed to see action before Japan's surrender.

Mitsubishi Ki-46 'Dinah'

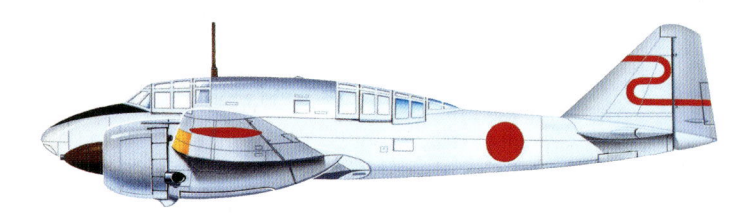

One of the finest reconnaissance aircraft of the war, the Ki-46's high performance saw it pressed into service in modified form as a B-29 interceptor.

The Ki-46 had first flown in November 1939 and in its original reconnaissance role had proved largely immune from interception. Even as late as 1945, the Ki-46-III was one of very few Japanese aircraft that could penetrate Allied airspace with relative impunity, although it lacked manoeuvrability and its rate of climb was poor, resulting in the shelving of a potential fighter adaptation in the summer of 1943.

The astonishing performance of the Ki-46 reconnaissance aircraft prompted the IJA to investigate an armed variant.

Mitsubishi Ki-46-III-KAI

Weight: 6228kg (13,730lb)
Dimensions: Length 11.48m (37ft 8in), Wingspan 14.70m (48ft 3in), Height 3.90m (12ft 6in)
Powerplant: Two 1119kW (1500hp) Mitsubishi Ha-112-II 14 cylinder air-cooled radial piston engines

Maximum speed: 610km/h (379mph)
Range: 2000km (1245 miles)
Ceiling: 10,500m (34,450ft)
Crew: 2
Armament: Two 20mm (0.79in) Ho-5 cannon in forward fuselage and one 37mm (1.46in) Ho-203 cannon obliquely mounted in centre fuselage

Opposite:
This major production version of the Ki-46-II served with the 76th *Dokuritsu Hiki Chutai* based in the East Indies in 1943.

Above:
This Ki-46-II is in the colours of the 51st *Dokuritsu Dai Shijugo Chutai*, in late 1941.

Below:
The dorsal 37mm (1.46in) Ho-203 cannon dominates the profile of this Ki-46-III-KAI. The aircraft proved a qualified success at best in combat.

However, the appearance of the B-29 over the home islands prompted a fresh look at the Ki-46 and it was felt that the aircraft's excellent endurance and performance at altitude might allow it to operate as an effective B-29 destroyer.

Ki-46-III

New-build Ki-46-IIIs were delivered directly to the 1st Army Air Arsenal at Tachikawa where a new nose equipped with two 20mm (0.79in) cannon replaced the extensively glazed cockpit. In the place of the fuselage fuel tank a single 37mm (1.46in) cannon was mounted, firing obliquely forward and upward. The first conversion, designated Ki-46-III-KAI, flew in October 1944 and around 200 aircraft were produced which were operated by several units. In service, the Ki-46-III-KAI proved disappointing, the oblique 37mm (1.46in) cannon proved ineffective and the Ki-46's structure, which had never been designed for fighter operations, proved unable to withstand much punishment.

Nakajima J1N1 *Gekko* 'Irving'

Conceived as a heavy fighter, though it entered service as a reconnaissance aircraft, the J1N1 was subsequently converted into a night fighter, achieving some success in this role.

Nakajima's response to a 1938 Imperial Navy request for a long-range fighter to escort the G3M bomber, the prototype J1N1, although very heavily armed, was considered overweight. Two powered turrets were fitted for rear defence and these proved unwieldy, the aircraft was not very manoeuvrable and suffered problems with its geared engines and hydraulic systems.

This photograph shows the cockpit arrangement of the J1N1-C reconnaissance version of the type.

Nakajima J1N1-S *Gekko*

Weight: 8185kg (18,045lb)
Dimensions: Length 12.77m (41ft 11in), Wingspan 16.98m (55ft 9in), Height 4.56m (15ft 0in)
Powerplant: Two 840kW (1130hp) Nakajima NK1F Sakae 21 14 cylinder air-cooled radial piston engines

Maximum speed: 507km/h (315mph)
Range: 2545km (1581 miles)
Ceiling: 9320m (30,580ft)
Crew: 2
Armament: Four 20mm (0.79in) Type 99 cannon, mounted obliquely, two upward and two downward-firing

Opposite:
Serving with the 251st *Kokutai* in November 1943, this J1N1-C-KAI was based at Lakunai airfield, Rabaul.

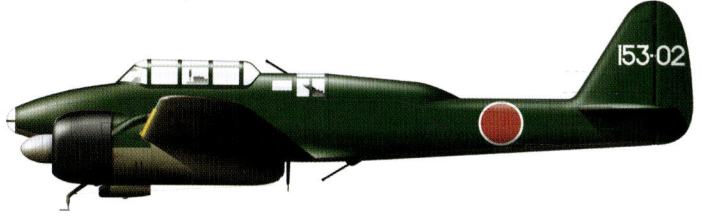

Above (both images):
The oblique cannon firing both upward and, unusually, downward are apparent on this J1N1-S of the 153rd *Kokutai* based at Mindanao in the Philippines. This aircraft was reportedly destroyed due to ramming a USAAF B-24 Liberator.

After this distinctly inauspicious start, Nakajima proposed a reconnaissance version with no turrets and ungeared *Sakae* 22 engines, and in this form the aircraft was accepted for production and entered service in late 1942.

Night fighter

The transformation of the *Gekko* ('Moonlight') into a night fighter first occurred at unit level when Commander Yasuna Kozono installed two 20mm (0.79in) cannon, firing obliquely upwards and forwards in the fuselage. This field-modified J1N1-C-KAI shot down two B-17s attacking air bases around Rabaul on 21 May 1943, prompting the Navy to order the type as the J1N1-S purpose-built night fighter. Initially successful against the B-17 and B-24, the J1N1 was harder pressed to intercept the B-29 due to its insufficient performance at altitude and lack of radar, though some late aircraft were fitted with a primitive airborne radar just before the end of the war. Some spectacular successes were nonetheless occasionally achieved with the J1N1, one crew reportedly shooting down five B-29s in one night.

Nakajima Ki-27 'Nate'

Quite possibly the most manoeuvrable monoplane fighter ever built, the Ki-27 replaced the Ki-10 biplane to become the Imperial Army's premier fighter type.

Nakajima had built a modern stressed skin monoplane with slotted flaps, a Hispano Suiza V-12 engine and retractable undercarriage as the Ki-12 in 1936 but the Army didn't want to rely on a foreign engine and felt it was lacking in manoeuvrability due to being overweight. Nakajima responded by introducing a simplified version with a radial engine, the Nakajima PE, which evolved into

These Ki-27s are in service with the puppet state of Manchukuo.

Nakajima Ki-27b

Weight: 1790kg (3946lb)
Dimensions: Length 7.53m (24ft 8in), Wingspan 11.31m (37ft 1in), Height 3.25m (10ft 8in)
Powerplant: One 530kW (710hp) Nakajima Ha-1 Kotobuki Otsu (Ha-1b) 9-cylinder air-cooled radial piston engine

Maximum speed: 470km/h (290mph)
Range: 627km (390 miles)
Ceiling: 12,250m (40,190ft)
Crew: 1
Armament: Two 7.7mm (0.303in) Type 89 machine guns; up to four 25kg (55lb) bombs under wings

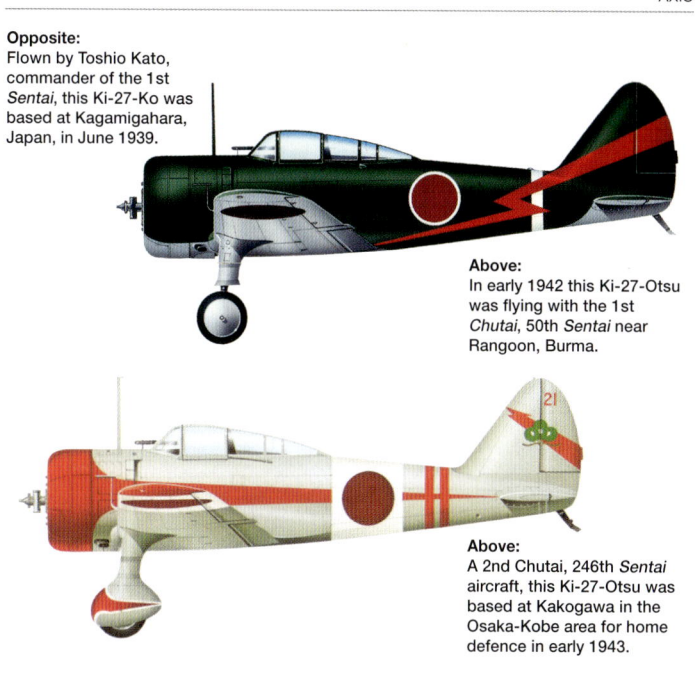

Opposite:
Flown by Toshio Kato, commander of the 1st *Sentai*, this Ki-27-Ko was based at Kagamigahara, Japan, in June 1939.

Above:
In early 1942 this Ki-27-Otsu was flying with the 1st *Chutai*, 50th *Sentai* near Rangoon, Burma.

Above:
A 2nd Chutai, 246th *Sentai* aircraft, this Ki-27-Otsu was based at Kakogawa in the Osaka-Kobe area for home defence in early 1943.

the mass-produced Ki-27. Making its first flight in October 1936, the Ki-27 was subsequently the main Japanese fighter during the undeclared war with the Soviet Union known as the Nomonhan Incident and during this campaign Japanese pilots claimed 1340 aircraft shot down. Despite this figure representing three times the entire number of Soviet aircraft in the theatre and thus representing a considerable overclaim, it was clear that the Ki-27 had proved highly successful.

By the outbreak of World War II, the Ki-27 was in the process of being replaced by the Ki-43 but was regularly encountered by Allied aircraft in the opening months of the conflict, including in clashes with the American Volunteer Group in China. Thereafter utilized as an advanced trainer, Ki-27s were pressed back into combat service in the closing stages of the war due to a shortage of modern aircraft and suffered severe losses. Eventually many were fitted with up to 500kg (1100lb) of explosives and expended in *kamikaze* attacks.

Nakajima Ki-43 *Hayabusa* 'Oscar'

The most produced combat aircraft of the Imperial Army, the Ki-43 retained the exceptional manoeuvrability of the Ki-27 and became the most numerous Imperial Army combat aircraft of the war.

The prototype of the Ki-43, first flown in January 1939, displayed poor manoeuvrability and proved barely faster than the Ki-27. A rigorous weight-saving programme, coupled with the adoption of the 'butterfly' flap, to increase lift in tight turns, transformed the agility of the aircraft and it entered service in June 1941. Encountered everywhere the Imperial Japanese Army Air Service (IJAAF)

A Ki-43-II-Otsu of the 2nd *Chutai*, 25th *Sentai*, taxies at its base in China.

Nakajima Ki-43-IIb *Hayabusa*

Weight: 2925kg (6449lb)
Dimensions: Length 8.92m (29ft 3in), Wingspan 10.84m (35ft 7in), Height 3.27m (10ft 9in)
Powerplant: One 970kW (1300hp) Nakajima Ha-115 14-cylinder air-cooled radial piston engine

Maximum speed: 530km/h (330mph)
Range: 1760km (1090 miles)
Ceiling: 11,200m (36,700ft)
Crew: 1
Armament: Two 12.7mm (0.5in) Ho-103 machine guns in the forward fuselage; up to 500kg (1100lb) bombload

Opposite:
Impressive unit markings adorn this Ki-43-I-Hei of the 1st *Chutai*, 50th *Sentai*, based at Tokorozawa in June 1942.

Above:
Ki-43-40 of the Manchukuo Army Air Corps based at Mukden (now Shenyang) in 1944. The inscription on the fuselage records that this aircraft was paid for by a donor.

Below:
Based at Chiang Mai in Thailand, this Ki-43-I-Hei flew with the 64th *Sentai* in March 1942 during the first Japanese attempt to cut off allied forces in Burma and India from China.

maintained a presence, the *Hayabusa* ('Peregrine Falcon') was often referred to by Allied aviators as the 'Army Zero', and followed the same design philosophy, possibly to an even greater extent than the more advanced Navy aircraft, wherein manoeuvrability and light weight were of paramount importance.

Weak armour

As such the Ki-43 possessed scarcely any protection for the pilot or fuel tanks and a structure that was vulnerable to gunfire. By contrast its own firepower was weak. Nonetheless, during the early stages of the war, the Ki-43 established an excellent record but as Allied pilots learned not to engage it in a classic turning dogfight the *Hayabusa* began to suffer, though like the Zero its incredible manoeuvrability made it a potentially dangerous opponent in the right hands until the end of the conflict. Unlike most Japanese aircraft, a few Ki-43s were used for a time in the postwar period, notably by French forces fighting the Viet Minh and by Indonesia against the Dutch.

Nakajima Ki-44 *Shoki* 'Tojo'

Despite resembling the Ki-43, the Ki-44 represented a departure from contemporary Japanese fighter design and was built for maximum speed and rate of climb in preference to manoeuvrability.

Making its maiden flight in August 1940, the Ki-44 possessed an unheralded wing loading for a Japanese fighter and although the handling qualities of the aircraft were deemed acceptable, it was believed to be a difficult aircraft to fly and initially garnered an evil reputation due to its high stalling speed and lack of manoeuvrability. The requirement for the aircraft was a response to the air

A Ki-44 taxies to the flightline at Akeno flying school in early 1944. Both aircraft in the foreground have had their wing armament removed.

Nakajima Ki-44-II-Otsu *Shoki*

Weight: 2993kg (6598lb)
Dimensions: Length 8.84m (29ft 0in), Wingspan 9.45m (31ft 0in), Height 3.25m (10ft 8in)
Powerplant: One 1133kW (1,519hp) Nakajima Ha-109 14-cylinder air-cooled radial piston engine
Maximum speed: 605km/h (376mph)

Range: 1200km (750 miles)
Ceiling: 11,200m (36,700ft)
Crew: 1
Armament: Two 12.7mm (0.5in) Ho-103 machine guns in cowling and two Ho-103 machine guns in wings; optional provision for two 40mm (1.575in) Ho-301 cannon in wings

Opposite:
A pre-series Ki-44 of the 47th Independent *Chutai* in Malaya, January 1942. This unit introduced the *Shoki* to operationial service.

Above:
The white panel behind the *Hinomaru* denotes that this Ki-44-II-Otsu was assigned to home defence. The tail marking is a stylized rendition of the number 23, this aircraft serving with the 23rd *Sentai* in 1944.

Below:
This Ki-44-II-Otsu was part of the 47th *Sentai* based at Narimasu, Tokyo, in the summer of 1944.

combat experience during the Nomonhan Incident wherein the Ki-27 had been out-climbed and out-dived by the sturdy Polikarpov I-16. It was realized that a dedicated high-speed interceptor would be a valuable complement to the traditional highly manoeuvrable general-purpose fighters.

'Butterfly' combat flap

Power of manoeuvre was not completely ignored, however, as the Ki-44 was fitted with a 'butterfly' combat flap to improve its turning performance. In service, trepidation changed to respect as it was found that the Ki-44 was not only, as expected, considerably faster than any other Imperial Japanese Army Air Service (IJAAF) fighter but was also possessed of an outstanding roll rate and an exceptional gun platform. As the Army's best climbing fighter, the Ki-44 initially became its primary B-29 interceptor. In attacks against the Superfortress, if a pilot had failed to bring down a bomber and had expended all his ammunition, he was expected to ram the B-29. Reportedly, one *Shoki* pilot, Sergeant Fujimoto, brought down two B-29s by ramming and survived.

Nakajima Ki-84 *Hayate* 'Frank'

The finest fighter to serve Japan in numbers, the Ki-84 was crippled by an unreliable engine, poor build quality and inexperienced aircrew but still demonstrated exceptional performance.

When the superb *Hayate* ('Gale') appeared in China in mid 1944, Allied pilots found themselves facing a fighter with astonishing performance combined with a powerful armament and an ability to absorb battle damage as yet unknown in a Japanese aircraft. Development of the Ki-84 had begun in early 1942 with the aim of producing an aircraft that combined the manoeuvrability of the *Hayabusa*

Ki-84-I of the 101st *Sentai* start their engines prior to a mass defensive action in the latter part of 1944.

Nakajima Ki-84-Ia *Hayate*

Weight: 4170kg (9193lb)
Dimensions: Length 9.92m (32ft 7in), Wingspan 11.24m (36ft 10in), Height 3.385m (11ft 1in)
Powerplant: 1522kW (2041hp) Nakajima Homare Model Ha-45 18-cylinder air-cooled radial piston engine
Maximum speed: 687km/h (427mph)

Range: 2168km (1347 miles)
Ceiling: 11,826m (38,800ft)
Crew: 1
Armament: Two 12.7mm (0.5in) Ho-103 machine guns in nose and two 20mm (0.79in) Ho-5 cannon in wings; up to 500kg (1100lb) bombload under wings

Opposite:
This Ki-84 was assigned to the 183rd *Shimbu-tai* (Special Attack Group) based at Tatebayashi, Japan, in August 1945.

Above:
The *Shimbu-tai* units were formed specifically to undertake *kamikaze* missions. This Ki-84-I-Ko was on the strength of the 58th *Shimbu-tai* in August 1945.

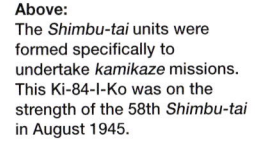

Below:
A colourful Ki-84-I-Ko of the Headquarters *Chutai* of the 29th *Sentai* based on Formosa in 1945. The *Sentai* emblem on the tail is a stylized breaking wave.

with the speed and climb of the *Shoki*. Designed by Yasumi Koyama, the Ki-84 utilized the new Nakajima *Homare* ('Honour') engine which promised power in the 1500kW (2000hp) class. Flown for the first time in April 1943, a large service trials batch of 83 aircraft was built and following enthusiastic reports from pilots the aircraft was put into full production.

Multirole aircraft

On its debut the Ki-84 could outclimb and outmanoeuvre any Allied aircraft then in service but it was also intended from the outset as a multirole combat aircraft, featuring hardpoints for a 250kg (550lb) bomb under each wing. Sadly for the Japanese, by early 1945 build quality was so poor that individual Ki-84s exhibited seriously differing performance. Hydraulics failed, the *Homare* engine proved troublesome and undercarriage legs even snapped on landing due to incorrectly tempered steel. Nonetheless, a Ki-84 in good condition gave even an inexperienced pilot a fighting chance against the latest Allied types until the very end of the war.

IAR 80 and 81

During the interwar era Romania made a concerted effort to develop a domestic aircraft production capability, resulting in the production of the long-serving IAR 80.

IAR built the Polish PZL P.24 and its French Gnome-Rhone engine under licence in the late 1930s but the design team at IAR, led by Ion Grosu, believed that they could build a better fighter. Utilizing the engine, rear fuselage and tail of the P.24, a new low-wing cantilever monoplane fighter with retractable undercarriage took shape as the IAR 80. Flying for the first time on 12 April 1939, the

This is an IAR 80B with heavier armament in a wing of greater span. Fifty-five examples of this improved variant were constructed.

IAR 80A

Weight: 2248kg (4956lb)
Dimensions: Length 9.22m (30ft 3in), Wingspan 9.09m (29ft 10in), Height 3.60m (11ft 10in)
Powerplant: One 764kW (1025hp) IAR K14 IVc32 1000A 14-cylinder two-row air-cooled radial piston engine (licence-built Gnome-

Rhône 14K Mistral Major)
Maximum speed: 495km/h (308mph)
Range: 1150km (715 miles)
Ceiling: 9500m (31,168ft)
Crew: 1
Armament: Six 7.92mm (0.312in) FN-Browning machine guns in wings

Opposite & right:
The IAR 80 provided Romania
with a workmanlike fighter when
alternative imported aircraft
were in short supply.

This rare colour photograph shows four IAR 80 fighters in flight.

aircraft proved superior to the gullwing PZL and an initial batch of 100 aircraft
was ordered.

Eastern Front

The IAR 80 possessed performance comparable to its contemporaries in 1939
but was not destined to see combat until the June 1941 invasion of the Soviet
Union, scoring its first victory on the opening day of the offensive. Against
Soviet aircraft the IAR 80 performed well, though it lacked firepower, and the IAR
80B introduced a six machine gun armament before a switch was made to two
20mm (0.79in) cannon and two machine guns in the IAR 80C. A dive bomber
variant, the IAR 81, was also developed when Romania was unable to obtain
Ju 87 Stukas from Germany. The IAR 80 was beginning to show its age by the
time it was called upon to deal with American attacks on the Ploiesti refinery in
1943 and 44 and the aircraft was replaced by Bf 109Gs in July 1944, though it
remained in second-line service until 1949.

INDEX

Picture Credits

Alamy: 14 (Vintage Mechanics), 20 (Maverick90), 24 & 26 (Interfoto), 40 (Sueddeutsche Zeitung), 54 (The Print Collector), 128 (Nigel J Clarke), 166 (The Picture Art Collection), 179 (Vintage Mechanics), 186 (The Picture Art Collection)

Alamy/Chronicle: 6, 12, 22, 30, 187, 190, 210, 214, 218

Amber Books: 10, 16, 18, 32, 38, 48, 49, 52, 56, 64, 65, 68-72 all, 76-86 all, 90, 98, 100, 108-120 all, 130, 132, 136, 140-148 all, 152-158 all, 162, 164, 174, 194, 198-202 all, 212, 216

ASL Photos: 42, 46, 58-62 all, 66, 123, 124, 134, 138, 160, 170, 172, 182, 196, 204, 206

Creative Commons Attribution-Share Alike 4.0 International Licence: 122

Getty Images: 36 & 51 (Sovfoto), 55 (Royal Air Force Museum), 88 & 102 (Corbis)

National Archives & Records Administration: 8/9

Naval History & Heritage Command: 94, 104, 106

Public Domain: 28, 34, 44, 50, 74, 96, 126, 129, 150, 168, 176, 178, 180, 184, 188, 192, 193, 208, 219

U.S. Air Force: 92